SRA

Algebra Readiness

English Learner Support Guide

McGraw Hill SRA

Columbus, OH

Author
Sharon Griffin
Professor of Education and
Adjunct Associate Professor of Psychology
Clark University
Worcester, Massachusetts

SRAonline.com

McGraw Hill SRA

Printed in the United States of America.

Send all inquiries to this address:
SRA/McGraw-Hill
4400 Easton Commons
Columbus, OH 43219

ISBN: 978-0-07-612416-9
MHID: 0-07-612416-9

1 2 3 4 5 6 7 8 9 DBH 13 12 11 10 09 08 07

The McGraw·Hill Companies

Contents

Contents

Contents

Introduction

This ***English Learner Support Guide*** provides both teacher and student support for ***Number Worlds*** to ensure access and ultimate success for all students in mathematics. The goal for English learners is to understand and use English in social as well as academic contexts so that they can fully participate in mathematics learning. This guide enables teachers to make the ***Number Worlds*** lessons as comprehensible as possible for students learning English, while also providing opportunities for oral and written responses.

Students must develop such receptive English-language skills as listening and reading and use them in turn to acquire vocabulary. Students must also develop their speaking skills to communicate what they have learned.

The following elements of English may present a particular challenge to students acquiring English:

- **English phonemes that may not exist in the student's home language**
- **Vocabulary**
- **Idioms and expressions**
- **Comprehension of written text**

The vocabulary instruction in the ***English Learner Support Guide*** will help students with general academic language development for receptive comprehension.

Academic Vocabulary words are words students need to know and be able to use for the upcoming week of ***Number Worlds***. These words are the words essential for comprehending the lesson and that students will encounter in future lessons. These words need to be taught explicitly, with multiple opportunities for students to practice using the words in context. In order for students to understand the mathematics lesson, they will need guidance in content-specific vocabulary. In addition, these meaningful vocabulary words will help the student's growth in English. The emphasis in the ***Number Worlds English Learner Support Guide*** is on developing the words needed for completing mathematics lessons with comprehension.

Resources

The ***Number Worlds*** program includes a variety of program materials designed to provide English Learner Support.

English Learner Support Guide

Teacher Edition

Student Edition

Vocabulary Cards

Each level of the ***English Learner Support Guide*** includes the following:

- Individual Oral Assessments
- Vocabulary Instruction
- Progress Monitoring
- Practice Pages for three levels of language acquisition
- Summative Assessments
- Blackline Masters
- Vocabulary Flashcards for additional practice

Stages of English Language Proficiency

An effective learning environment is an important goal of all teachers. In a supportive environment, all English learners have the opportunity to participate and to learn. The materials in this guide are designed to support students while they are acquiring English.

This guide provides direction in supporting students in three stages of English proficiency: Beginning, Intermediate, and Advanced. These three stages can be described in general terms as follows.

- **Beginning** Students identified at this level of English-language proficiency know little English and will probably have difficulty comprehending English. During this stage, students demonstrate dramatic growth as they progress from having no receptive or productive English to possessing a basic command of English. They are learning to comprehend and produce one- or two-word responses to questions and are moving to phrases and simple sentences using concrete and immediate topics and to interact in a limited fashion with text that has been taught. They progress to responding with increasing ease to more varied communication tasks using learned material, comprehending a sequence of information on familiar topics, producing basic statements and asking questions on familiar subjects, and interacting with a variety of print. Some basic errors are found in their use of English syntax and grammar.

- **Intermediate** Students who have reached the intermediate level of English-language proficiency have good comprehension of overall meaning and are beginning to demonstrate increased comprehension of specific details and concepts. They are learning to respond in expanded sentences, interact more independently with a variety of texts, and use newly acquired English vocabulary to communicate ideas orally and in writing. They demonstrate fewer errors in English grammar and syntax than at the Beginning level.

- **Early Advanced/Advanced** Students who are identified at this level of English-language proficiency demonstrate consistent comprehension of meaning, including implied and nuanced meaning, and are learning the use of idiomatic and figurative language. They are increasingly able to respond using detail in compound and complex sentences and to sustain conversations in English. They are able to use standard grammar with few errors and show understanding of conventions of formal and informal usage.

Academic Language Acquisition

English learners often sound fluent in conversation, which leads teachers to believe that they are completely proficient in English in all settings. Social conversation is often concrete, discussing events and subjects familiar to English learners. However, academic language, the language that allows students to discuss abstract concepts, employs sophisticated grammatical constructions. Proficiency in communication using academic language is important for the success of all students, including English learners.

Mathematics, like all content-area subjects, has a special language that helps students learn key concepts and discuss them with others. This academic language includes unique terminology to mathematics, as well as the signs and symbols that are used to convey common understandings. The academic language of mathematics is not usually encountered in social settings. It must be explicitly taught and practiced. One unique challenge to teachers of English learners is that students learning English may arrive at school for the first time in any grade level. This means that, at every grade level, teachers need to be prepared with a tool kit of strategies to accelerate language learning and to backfill skills that may have been taught and mastered by other students in previous grade levels.

Another challenge is that some students arrive with high levels of mathematics preparation. These students may know the mathematics, but now must learn the subject matter discourse in order to ask questions, read and comprehend the textbook, and otherwise participate in class.

Ways to Teach Vocabulary

The English Leaner Support in the ***Number Worlds Teacher Edition*** provides teachers with valuable tools to meet the needs of English learners. Often English learners understand the mathematics in a lesson but cannot communicate that understanding in English. The following are some strategies for teaching vocabulary that can be incorporated in any subject.

Real Objects and Realia: Because of the immediate result visuals have on learning language, when explaining a word such as *car*, the best approach is simply to show a real car. As an alternate to the real object, you can show realia. Realia are toy versions of real things, such as plastic eggs to substitute for real eggs, or in this case, a toy car to signify a real car. A large, clear picture of an automobile can also work if it is absolutely recognizable.

If, however, the student has had no experience with the item in the picture, more explanation might be needed. For example, if the word you are explaining is a zoo animal such as an ocelot and the students are not familiar with this animal, one picture might be insufficient. They might confuse this animal with a cat or any one of the feline species, such as a tiger. Seeing several clear pictures, then, of each individual type of common feline and comparing their similarities and differences might help clarify meaning in this particular instance. When students make a connection between their prior knowledge of the word *cat* with the new word *ocelot*, it validates their newly acquired knowledge, and thus they process learning more quickly.

Pictures: In many cases bringing real objects into the classroom is not practical. Supplement Big Book illustrations with visuals such as those found in the ***SRA Photo Library***, magazine pictures, and picture dictionaries. Videos, especially those that demonstrate an entire setting such as a farm or a zoo, or videos where different animals are highlighted in their natural habitat, for instance, might be helpful. You might also wish to turn off the sound to avoid a flood of language that students might not be able to understand. Since you want them to concentrate in the visual/word meaning correlation, leaving the sound on will take away meaning form the visual/interpretative connection. Students generally will be able to establish links more easily without sound, especially at the beginning of English language acquisition.

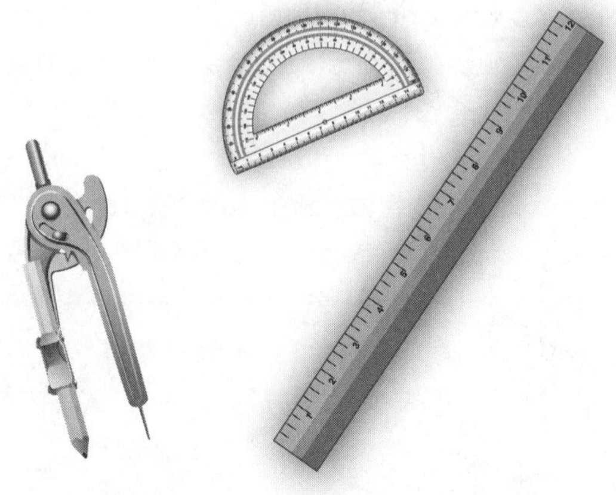

Using drawings that are sketchy, indistinct, or incomplete may be cryptic to students. When possible, select large, clear, and simple drawings that show entire objects, or use clear photos.

Graphic Organizers: Various kinds of graphic organizers and semantic maps can be very helpful, particularly with students who have attained Intermediate English-language proficiency and for moving students to higher levels of proficiency.

Pantomime: Language is learned through modeling within a communicative context. Pantomiming is one example of such a framework of communication. Some words, such as run or jump, are appropriate for pantomiming. You could use photos or picture cards for verbs like these, but demonstrating running and jumping is also necessary to solidify meaning. If students understand what you are trying to pantomime or if they recognize what it is you are striving to signify through your gestures or your facial expressions, they will more easily engage in the task of learning.

Getting Families of English Learners Involved

Family involvement is critical in a child's education. Do not let language be a barrier. Invite non-English speaking parents to help in the class by sending them a letter in their native language. A letter is a good way to begin the communication process. A sample letter in English is provided on page 135; the translations of the letter can be found on pages 136 through 141.

Sheltered Instruction

When English learners work in the core-content areas, they face the challenge of both the new concept load and the new language load. Sheltered instruction designs lesson delivery to take advantage of student language strengths and techniques that do not rely solely on telling, but on doing so that students see, hear, and experience the new concept along with the new language. ***Algebra Readiness*** employs the following sheltered instruction strategies throughout the program.

Accessing Prior Knowledge Sheltered Instruction begins with accessing students' prior knowledge to determine what they already know and how much background building may be necessary. The lessons in ***Algebra Readiness*** begin with Warm Up exercises and follow up with discussions and activities that provoke students to think about and share what they already know, allowing the teacher to diagnose where gaps may exist.

Modeling Demonstrating new math skills and concepts is a crucial developmental focus of Number Worlds, and it is one of the key strategies of Sheltered Instruction. When new concepts and skills are introduced, prior knowledge provides scaffolding as students see their teacher use manipulatives, hear appropriate terminology, and practice setting.

Checking for Understanding Sheltered Instruction involves interaction with the teacher, including checking for understanding along the way. When students are in the early stages of English language acquisition, they may not always be the first to answer a question or be able to fully express their ideas in speech or in writing. ***Algebra Readiness*** builds in many modes of checking comprehension throughout the lesson so that all students can show what they know. For example, a lesson may suggest that students can use a signal, such as thumbs-up or thumbs-down, to indicate their understanding. In this way, English learners access the core concepts but do not have to rely only on English expression to show what they know or where they need additional help.

Explicit Instruction The step-by-step instruction in ***Algebra Readiness*** is carefully structured to lead students to understanding the concepts. Built into the teaching are explanations of new terms and skills. It provides for plenty of repetition and revisiting of these concepts using the vocabulary so that students have ample modeling before they are expected to use these terms themselves.

Math Games English learners need to practice their new language in authentic settings rather than with drills that do not capture the language tasks students need to perform in school. Language learning can be a high-anxiety experience because the nature of the learning means that the speaker will make many mistakes. This can be profoundly difficult in front of one's peers or in answering individual questions in front of the whole class. Working in pairs and groups allows English learners a way to understand in a low-anxiety environment and allows more learning to take place.

A big part of the practice built into ***Algebra Readiness*** is in the form of learning games. In addition to being fun and motivating, math games provide English learners additional opportunity to practice. Vocabulary is woven into appropriate language repetition and revisiting skills and strategies. In addition, these specially designed games model strategic thinking so that even students at beginning levels of proficiency learn strategy and can demonstrate strategic, higher-level thinking.

Preview/Review Technique A quick review of the key concepts in the primary language allows students to converse with peers who speak the same primary language to be sure concepts are clear. If the teacher or an aide speaks the primary language of the students, this provides the additional benefit of answering questions and elaborating on the key concepts for students.

One of the true benefits of Preview/Review is that students focus on the lesson in English rather than waiting to alternate with the primary language translation. The teacher can use the English words in every lesson as an example of what the primary language preview should include.

Strategies for Teaching English Learners

Strategy 1

Build a Classroom Environment to Ensure Success

- Make sure students see the names of objects. Label everything.
- Speak clearly without distorting language.
- Learn words in your students' home language. Share them with the class, introducing their culture to all.
- Assign helper duties to your English Learners to ensure they feel part of the class.
- Make sure to praise students often, creating opportunities for success.

Strategy 2

Build on prior knowledge.

- Give English learners a list of vocabulary words before they use the words in lessons. Provide a dictionary to help students learn the words.
- Use Venn diagrams, KWL charts (What I Know, What I Want to Know, What I Learned), and other graphic organizers to help students relate words.
- Allow discussion before assigning a lesson to help students build linguistic skills.

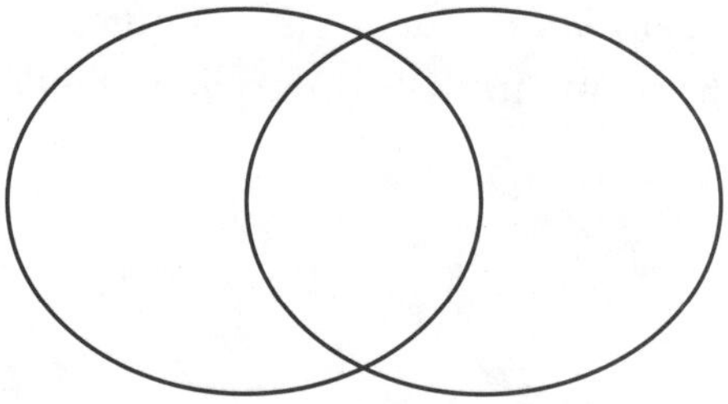

Use these Venn diagrams to sort objects and characteristics.
English Learner Support Guide, Level D

Strategy 3

Incorporate culture at every opportunity.

- Provide cultural background for students. Often, text assumes cultural familiarity.
- Include relevant examples whenever possible. Comparing situations to those in another culture may help.

Strategy 4
Give visual clues.

- Take vocabulary words out of the written context and provide visuals clue to help build students understanding. Use pictures, charts, and graphic organizers as clues.
- Use graphic organizers, such as Venn Diagrams, to build visual associations.

	Number of sides	Number of angles or corners	Number of right angles	Notes
Square				
Triangle				
Circle				
Rectangle				

Use this shape chart to identify different shapes.
English Learner Support Guide, Level D

Strategy 5
Simplify grammatical structures.

- Repeat, repeat, repeat. Use the same sentence structure when giving directions.
- Summarize lessons in simpler form.
- Introduce one concept per sentence.
- Simplify sentences, but include essential academic vocabulary.
- Use the subject/verb/object sentence structure.
- Use the active, not passive, voice.

Strategy 6
Teach vocabulary while teaching the lesson.

- Model pronunciation.
- Create an environment where students feel safe to make a mistake.
- Explain idiomatic language and word meanings.

Strategy 7
Teach for depth of understanding.

- Develop a clear understanding of content in depth.
- Focus on learning a few concepts well to give English learners a greater opportunity for success.

Strategy 8
Teach study skills.

- Guide learners to use text resources: tables of contents, glossaries, indexes, captions, and stylized text.
- Help students who cannot read the text use words and pictures to categorize the text.
- Make sure that learners realize that textbooks are written to provide information.
- Organize students into pairs as learning companions.
- Provide students with categorical word lists.
- Create topic outlines.

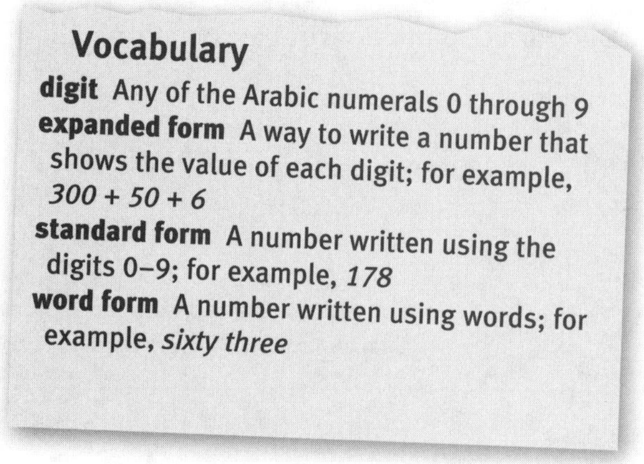
Vocabulary
digit Any of the Arabic numerals 0 through 9
expanded form A way to write a number that shows the value of each digit; for example, *300 + 50 + 6*
standard form A number written using the digits 0–9; for example, *178*
word form A number written using words; for example, *sixty three*

***English Learner Support Guide*, Level F**

Strategy 9
Use manipulatives.

- Involve English learners with hands-on activities.
- Encourage students to construct, graph, measure, and experiment.
- Encourage discussion while students use hands-on materials.

Strategy 10
Inform and adapt instruction.

- Ask questions based on students English proficiency level.
- Monitor progress daily.
- Allow students to show their knowledge in different ways, especially by using visual aids, graphs, and drawings.

Progress Monitoring

If . . . students need additional practice using coordinate grids,

Then . . . use a city map using coordinates to find a point. Using a map of your school or municipality will give English learners additional practice recognizing and pronouncing street names where they live.

English Learner Support Guide, Level H

Strategy 11
Use cooperative learning.

- Use the buddy system to help learners work efficiently. English learners working cooperatively make substantial learning gains.
- Include English learners in group work. Even if their comprehension is low, they will learn academic vocabulary and skills.

Lesson Routines

1 Warm Up

Begin every day with the lesson **Warm Up** with the entire group. These short activities are used in a whole-group format at the beginning of each day's lesson.

Warm Up is an essential component because it helps students to preview vocabulary they will use in the **Engage** activities. It also gives students daily opportunities to sharpen their vocabulary understanding.

2 Engage

Engage includes intensive vocabulary instruction. Suggestions are included to introduce vocabulary. Guided discussion, game demonstrations, and strategy building activities develop

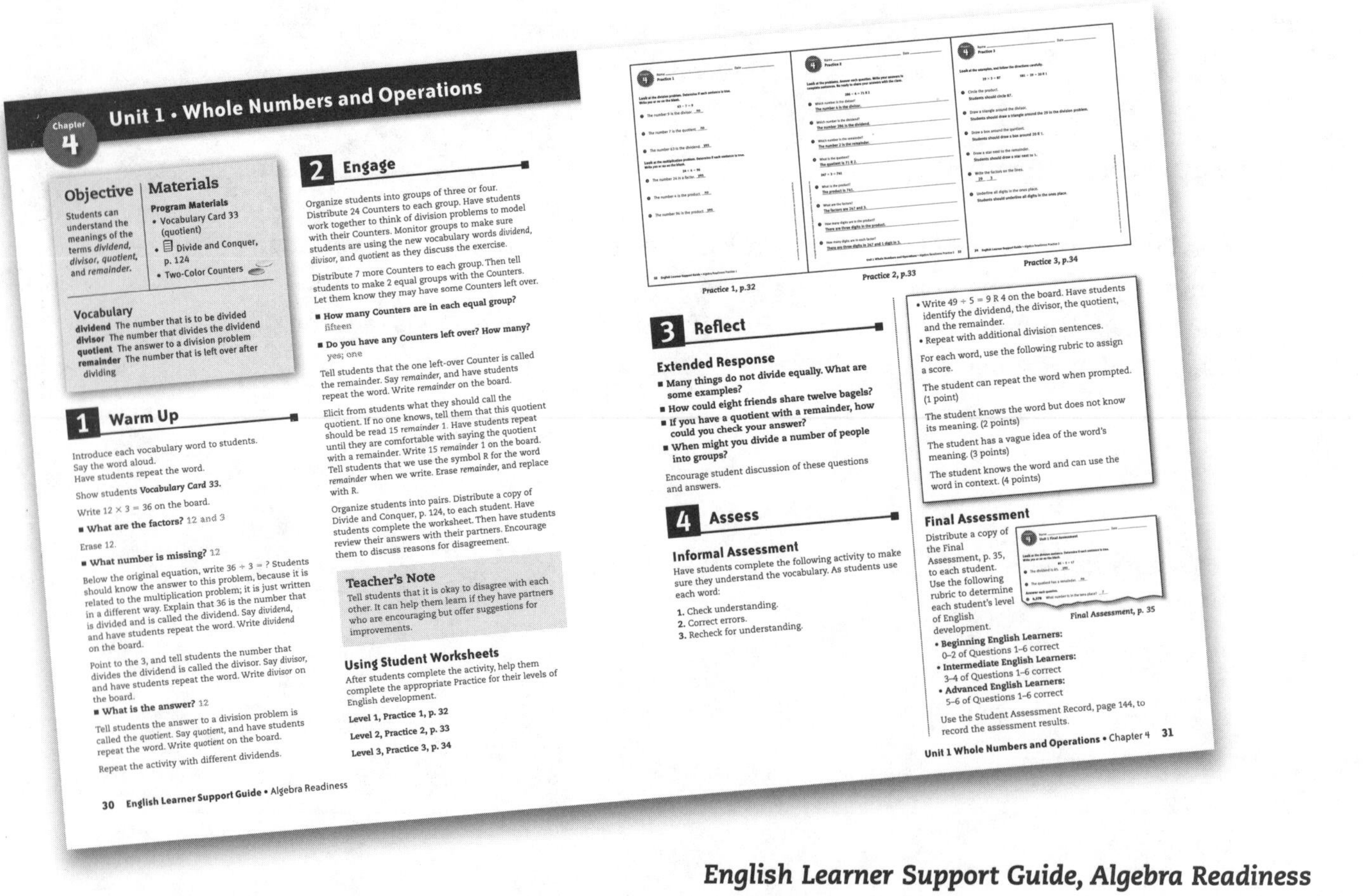

Chapter 4

Unit 1 • Whole Numbers and Operations

Objective

Students can understand the meanings of the terms *dividend*, *divisor*, *quotient*, and *remainder*.

Materials

Program Materials

- Vocabulary Card 33 (quotient)
- Divide and Conquer, p. 124
- Two-Color Counters

Vocabulary

dividend The number that is to be divided
divisor The number that divides the dividend
quotient The answer to a division problem
remainder The number that is left over after dividing

1 Warm Up

Introduce each vocabulary word to students.
Say the word aloud.
Have students repeat the word.

Show students **Vocabulary Card 33.**

Write 12 × 3 = 36 on the board.

- **What are the factors?** 12 and 3

Erase 12.

- **What number is missing?** 12

Below the original equation, write 36 ÷ 3 = ? Students should know the answer to this problem, because it is related to the multiplication problem; it is just written in a different way. Explain that 36 is the number that is divided and is called the dividend. Say *dividend*, and have students repeat the word. Write *dividend* on the board.

Point to the 3, and tell students the number that divides the dividend is called the divisor. Say *divisor*, and have students repeat the word. Write *divisor* on the board.

- **What is the answer?** 12

Tell students the answer to a division problem is called the *quotient*. Say *quotient*, and have students repeat the word. Write *quotient* on the board.

Repeat the activity with different dividends.

2 Engage

Organize students into groups of three or four. Distribute 24 Counters to each group. Have students work together to think of division problems to model with their Counters. Monitor groups to make sure students are using the new vocabulary words *dividend*, *divisor*, and *quotient* as they discuss the exercise.

Distribute 7 more Counters to each group. Then tell students to make 2 equal groups with the Counters. Let them know they may have some Counters left over.

- **How many Counters are in each equal group?** fifteen
- **Do you have any Counters left over? How many?** yes; one

Tell students that the one left-over Counter is called the remainder. Say *remainder*, and have students repeat the word. Write *remainder* on the board.

Elicit from students what they should call the quotient. If no one knows, tell them that this quotient should be read 15 *remainder* 1. Have students repeat until they are comfortable with saying the quotient with a remainder. Write 15 *remainder* 1 on the board. Tell students that we use the symbol R for the word *remainder* when we write. Erase *remainder*, and replace with R.

Organize students into pairs. Distribute a copy of Divide and Conquer, p. 124, to each student. Have students complete the worksheet. Then have students review their answers with their partners. Encourage them to discuss reasons for disagreement.

Teacher's Note

Tell students that it is okay to disagree with each other. It can help them learn if they have partners who are encouraging but offer suggestions for improvements.

Using Student Worksheets

After students complete the activity, help them complete the appropriate Practice for their levels of English development.

Level 1, Practice 1, p. 32
Level 2, Practice 2, p. 33
Level 3, Practice 3, p. 34

30 English Learner Support Guide • Algebra Readiness

Practice 1, p.32

Practice 2, p.33

Practice 3, p.34

3 Reflect

Extended Response

- **Many things do not divide equally. What are some examples?**
- **How could eight friends share twelve bagels?**
- **If you have a quotient with a remainder, how could you check your answer?**
- **When might you divide a number of people into groups?**

Encourage student discussion of these questions and answers.

4 Assess

Informal Assessment

Have students complete the following activity to make sure they understand the vocabulary. As students use each word:

1. Check understanding.
2. Correct errors.
3. Recheck for understanding.

- Write 49 ÷ 5 = 9 R 4 on the board. Have students identify the dividend, the divisor, the quotient, and the remainder.
- Repeat with additional division sentences.

For each word, use the following rubric to assign a score.

The student can repeat the word when prompted. (1 point)

The student knows the word but does not know its meaning. (2 points)

The student has a vague idea of the word's meaning. (3 points)

The student knows the word and can use the word in context. (4 points)

Final Assessment

Distribute a copy of the Final Assessment, p. 35, to each student. Use the following rubric to determine each student's level of English development.

Final Assessment, p. 35

- **Beginning English Learners:** 0–2 of Questions 1–6 correct
- **Intermediate English Learners:** 3–4 of Questions 1–6 correct
- **Advanced English Learners:** 5–6 of Questions 1–6 correct

Use the Student Assessment Record, page 144, to record the assessment results.

Unit 1 Whole Numbers and Operations • Chapter 4 31

English Learner Support Guide, Algebra Readiness

student understanding. Before beginning the activity, familiarize yourself with the lesson vocabulary, while making sure materials are available for student use. Introduce the activity, and use discussion to help students explore the lesson vocabulary.

Classroom discussion is encouraged in every lesson. Rules for classroom discussion established at the beginning of the year make each lesson more meaningful and promote listening and speaking skills. The following are some helpful ways to facilitate classroom discussion.

- **Pay attention to others.** Give your full attention to the person who is speaking. This includes looking at the speaker and nodding to show that you understand.
- **Wait for speakers to answer and complete their thoughts.** Sometimes teachers and other students get impatient and move on to ask someone else before someone has a chance to think and speak. Giving students time to answer is a vital part of teaching for understanding.
- **Listen.** Let yourself finish listening before you begin to speak. You can't listen if you are busy thinking about what you want to say next.
- **Respect speakers.** Take turns and make sure that everyone gets a chance to speak and that no one dominates the conversation.
- **Build on others' ideas.** Make connections, draw analogies, or expand on the idea.
- **Ask questions.** Asking questions of another speaker shows that you were listening. Ask for clarification or an explanation if you are not sure you understand what the speaker has said. It is a good idea to repeat what the speaker has said in your own words to be sure your understanding is correct.

Using Student Worksheets

In every week of the program, levels D and up, you will assign student practice based on each student's level of English Proficiency. Practice 1 worksheets require little or no language other than vocabulary words. Practice 2 worksheets require some reading comprehension and writing skills. Practice 3 worksheets assume greater English-language proficiency. At each level of English proficiency, the worksheet pages help students learn to use in context the vocabulary presented throughout the week.

3 Reflect

Reflect is a vital part of the lesson that offers ways to help students summarize and reflect on their understanding of lesson vocabulary. When students talk about their thinking, they engage in mathematical generalizing and communicating. Allowing students to discuss what they did during an activity helps build mathematical reasoning and also develops social skills, such as taking turns, listening, and speaking. At the designated time, have students stop working and direct their attention to reflecting on the lesson.

Use the suggested questions in **Reflect**, or have students

- summarize ideas using the lesson vocabulary.
- compare how the lesson vocabulary words are like and unlike.
- describe where they have seen or can apply the lesson vocabulary in the world outside of school.
- identify related vocabulary.

The following are good questions to develop vocabulary:

- How do you know?
- How did you figure that out?
- Why?
- Tell me about...
- How is that the same?
- How is that different?

4 Assess

Assess helps you use informal and formal assessments to summarize and analyze evidence of student understanding and plan for differentiating instruction.

Progress Monitoring

Informal daily assessments evaluate students' vocabulary proficiency. **Warm-Up** exercises and **Engage** activities can be used for day-to-day observation and assessment of how well each student is learning skills and grasping concepts. The **Engage** activities allow you to watch students using vocabulary under conditions more natural to them than most classroom activities. **Warm-Up** exercises allow you to see individual responses, give immediate feedback, and involve the entire class.

Simple rubrics enable teachers to assay their observations. Individual scores can later be recorded in the Student Assessment Record or in ***eAssess*** to help provide a more complete view of student proficiency.

Formal Assessment

Final Assessments provide formal assessments for each week of the ***Number Worlds*** program. These assessments provide information about the level of understanding of each of the vocabulary words taught in the ***Number Worlds*** program. They also help teachers to continually monitor the student's level of English language proficiency in the context of content-area mathematics.

Whole Numbers and Operations

Unit at a Glance

In this unit, students will learn the vocabulary associated with ***Number Worlds***, Algebra Readiness, Whole Numbers and Operations. In this unit, students will construct and identify the place value for each digit in numbers to 10,000 and learn to perform the operations of addition, subtraction, multiplication, and division on those numbers. Before beginning the unit, assess students' general knowledge of math and vocabulary using the Individual Oral Assessment on page 23.

How Students Learn Vocabulary

Using visuals has an immediate impact on learning language. For this unit, it will be helpful to have base-ten blocks, Counters, Play Money, and Number Cubes on hand so students can visualize the reality of the operations they will be conducting.

Whenever possible, have students work in pairs or small groups to maximize fluency practice. Encourage them to incorporate the new vocabulary in their pair work.

Academic Vocabulary Taught in Unit 1

Chapter 1	Chapter 2	Chapter 3	Chapter 4
greater than Larger in number or measure **less than** Smaller in number or measure **place value** The value of a digit in a numeral, written in standard notation, according to its position, or place, in the numeral	**algorithm** A step-by-step procedure for carrying out a computation or solving a problem **digit** Any of the ten Arabic numerals from 0 through 9 **subtract** To take away, as in one quantity from another	**factor** A number that is multiplied to get a product; for example: 3 (multiplier) $\times$ 5 (multiplicand) $=$ 15 (product) **multiply** To find the product of a number that is repeatedly added to itself ($4 + 4 + 4 = 3 \times 4 = 12$) **product** The result of multiplying two or more numbers (factors)	**dividend** The number that is to be divided **divisor** The number that divides the dividend **quotient** The answer to a division problem **remainder** The number that is left over after dividing

Math at Home

Give one copy of the appropriate Letter to Home, pages 135 through 141, to each student to take home on the day you begin this unit. Encourage students to share and complete the activity with their caregivers.

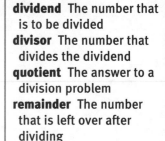

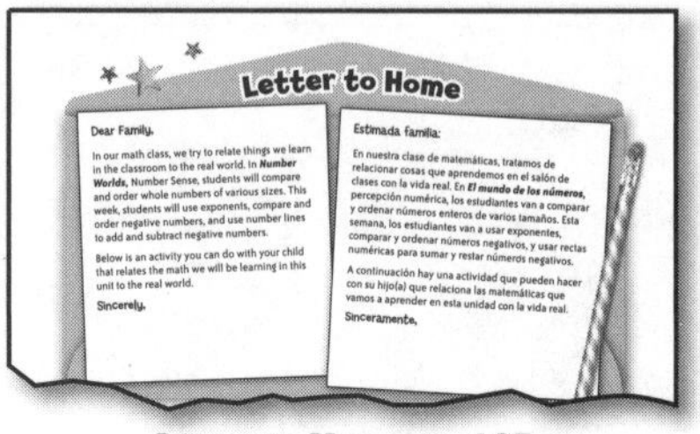

Letter to Home, p. 135

Unit 1 Individual Oral Assessment

Directions: Read each question to the student, and record his or her oral responses. Some questions have teacher directions. Teacher directions are indicated in italics. Allow students to use pencil and paper to work their responses.

1. Is this a **quotient**? *Write* 30 ÷ 6 = 5 *on a piece of paper. Point to the* 6. **no**
2. Is this a **dividend**? *Point to the* 30. **yes**
3. Is there a **remainder**? *Use the same division sentence above.* **no**
4. Is this a **factor**? *Write* 4 × 9 = 36 *on a piece of paper. Point to* 36. **no**
5. What is the **place value** of the 3? *Write* 5,348 *on a piece of paper.* **hundreds**
6. How many **digits** are there in the number 275? **3**
7. What is the **product**? *Write* 6 × 8 *on a piece of paper.* **48**
8. What is the **place value** of the 2? *Write the number* 523 *on a piece of paper.* **tens**
9. Which of these requires an **algorithm**? *Write* 13 − 7 = 6 *and* 617 *on a piece of paper.* **13 − 7 = 6**
10. What are the **factors** of 27? **1, 3, 9, 27**
11. What is the **product**? *Write* 3 × 7 *on a piece of paper.* **21**
12. What is the **quotient**? *Write* 42 ÷ 7 *on a piece of paper.* **6**
13. What is the **quotient** with the **remainder**? *Write* 39 ÷ 6 *on a piece of paper.* **6 R 3**

- **Beginning English Learners:** 0–3 of Questions 1–10 correct
- **Intermediate English Learners:** 4–7 of Questions 1–10 correct
- **Advanced English Learners:** 8–10 of questions 1–10 correct
- If the student is able to answer Questions 11–13, then he or she can understand the mathematics taught in this unit, but may still have difficulty with the academic vocabulary.

Use the Student Assessment Record, page 144, to record the assessment results.

Objective

Students can understand the meanings of the terms *greater than, less than,* and *place value.*

Materials

Program Materials

- Number Construction Mat, *Teacher Edition,* p. B1
- Place Value, p. 123

Additional Materials

Base-ten blocks

Vocabulary

greater than Larger in number or measure
less than Smaller in number or measure
place value The value of a digit in a numeral, written in standard notation, according to its position, or place, in the numeral

1 Warm Up

Introduce each vocabulary word to students.
Say the word aloud.
Have students repeat the word.

Organize students into pairs. Distribute a handful of the unit cubes from the base-ten blocks set to each pair of students. Have students organize the cubes into a group of seven cubes and a group of nine cubes. Have them set aside any extra cubes.

- **Which pile has more cubes?** the set of 9
- **Which pile has fewer cubes?** the set of 7

Tell students that because nine is more than seven, we say that nine is *greater than* seven. Say *greater than* again, and have students repeat the term. Write *greater than* on the board. Repeat for *less than.*

Ask additional comparison questions to check students' concept of *greater than* and *less than.*

2 Engage

Write 5 on the board. Point to the number.

- **What number is this?** five
- **How many ones are there in five?** five

If no one can answer this question, then write 1 + 1 + 1 + 1 + 1 on the board. Once you begin to write, students may catch on. After you have done this, ask the question again. Point to the 5, say *ones place,* and have students repeat the term. Write *ones* above the number on the board. Demonstrate *ones place* with the unit cubes from the base-ten blocks.

Change the number 5 on the board to the number 45. Point to the 5.

- **What number is this?** 5
- **How many ones are there in 5?** 5

Point to the four.

- **What number is this?** four; accept forty-five
- **How many tens are there?** four

If no one can answer this question, then write 10 + 10 + 10 + 10 on the board. Again, students may catch on once you begin to write. After you have done this, ask the question again. Point to the 4, say *tens place,* and have students repeat the term. Write *tens* above the number on the board. Have students say the number. Demonstrate *tens place* with the rods from the base-ten blocks.

Continue this process until students have learned the place values up to *thousands* for the number 8,345. Tell students they have just learned the place value for each digit in this large number. Say *place value,* and have students repeat the term. Write *place value* on the board. Use 100 flats and 1,000 cubes from the base-ten blocks to demonstrate the place values of the digits 8 and 3.

Organize students into pairs. Have partners practice naming place value by saying large numbers. If they have trouble, distribute a copy of Number Construction Mat, ***Teacher Edition,*** p. B1, to each pair of students. Have them enter the number on the number construction mat and read from that.

Distribute a copy of Place Value, p. 123, to each student. Have students complete the worksheet with their partners.

Teacher's Note

Concept checking is an important part of teaching to English learners. When introducing vocabulary, ask questions to determine whether students understand the meanings of words and ideas. Ask concept-check questions to individual students and occasionally to the whole group.

Be aware that in some countries, the use of commas and decimal points is reversed. For example, in the United States, the number four thousand three hundred twenty-two and 5 tenths is written as 4,322.5. In Indonesia, however, it is written as 4.322,5.

Progress Monitoring

If . . . students struggle to understand place value,	**Then . . .** allow them to practice representing numbers using base-ten blocks.

3 Reflect

Extended Response

- **Why do we use commas to write large numbers?**
- **Why is place value important?**
- **Why do we use the words *ones, tens, hundreds,* and so on to talk about place value?**

Encourage student discussion of these questions and answers.

Progress Monitoring

If . . . students struggle with saying the numbers aloud,	**Then . . .** have them write each number in words first.

4 Assess

Informal Assessment

Have students complete the activity below to make sure they understand the vocabulary. As students use each word:

1. Check understanding.
2. Correct errors.
3. Recheck for understanding.

- Write the number 7,324 on the board. Have students identify the place value of each digit.
- Have students define *greater than* and *less than* in their own words.

For each word, use the following rubric to assign a score.

The student can repeat the word when prompted. (1 point)

The student knows the word but does not know its meaning. (2 points)

The student has a vague idea of the word's meaning. (3 points)

The student knows the word and can use the word in context. (4 points)

Objective

Students can understand the meanings of the terms *digit*, *subtract*, and *algorithm*.

Materials

Program Materials

Two-Color Counters 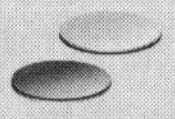

Vocabulary

algorithm A step-by-step procedure for carrying out a computation or solving a problem

digit Any of the ten Arabic numerals from 0 through 9

subtract To take away, as in one quantity from another

1 Warm Up

Introduce each vocabulary word to students.
Say the word aloud.
Have students repeat the word.

Review place value with students. Organize students into four groups; for example, each row of desks could be one group. Assign each group as *ones, tens, hundreds,* or *thousands.* Write the number 3,792 on the board. As you point to each digit, students whose group represents that place value should raise their hands and say the place value. For example, if you point to the number 7, the hundreds group should raise hands and say *hundreds.*

Continue the activity until students have a firm understanding of the values. Change numbers and switch groups.

2 Engage

Have a volunteer count from zero through nine as you write these digits on the board. Tell students that these numbers are called digits and that digits make up any number. The number 145, for example, is made of the digits 1, 4, and 5. Say *digit,* and have students repeat the word. Write *digit* on the board.

Show students three Counters.

- **How many Counters do I have?** 3

As students watch, take one Counter away.

- **Now how many Counters do I have?** 2
- **Is that greater than or less than three?** less than

Tell students that when you take numbers away, you subtract the number. Say *subtract,* and have students repeat the word. Write *subtract* on the board, then write $3 - 1 = 2$ on the board.

Point to the subtraction sentence you wrote on the board. Tell students that a step-by-step procedure for carrying out a computation or solving a problem is called an algorithm. Say *algorithm,* and have students repeat the word. Write *algorithm* on the board.

Have students work with a partner to practice using subtraction algorithms. Have students say aloud each subtraction sentence. Monitor each pair, and praise students for their use of new vocabulary.

Teacher's Note

Model and practice the sentence structure needed for talking about subtraction problems with English learners. Make sure to use the word *minus.* When you say aloud each number sentence, ask one or more students to repeat the structure after you. Then remind students to use this structure when saying their number sentences.

Progress Monitoring

If . . . students confuse *digits* and *place value,*

Then . . . model building a number using various digits for each place value to illustrate that the place value remains in the same position within a number.

3 Reflect

Extended Response

- **What is an algorithm?**
- **How is an algorithm like a recipe?**
- **How are digits and place value different?**
- **What are some words we use to talk about subtraction?**

Encourage student discussion of these questions and answers.

Progress Monitoring	
If . . . students hesitate to participate in open discussion,	**Then . . .** have them hold discussions in pairs or small groups.

4 Assess

Informal Assessment

Have students complete the activity below to make sure they understand the vocabulary. As students use each word:

1. Check understanding.
2. Correct errors.
3. Recheck for understanding.

Have students define *algorithm* and describe a subtraction algorithm in their own words.

For each word, use the following rubric to assign a score.

The student can repeat the word when prompted. (1 point)

The student knows the word but does not know its meaning. (2 points)

The student has a vague idea of the word's meaning. (3 points)

The student knows the word and can use the word in context. (4 points)

Chapter 3

Unit 1 • Whole Numbers and Operations

Objective

Students can understand the meanings of the terms *factor*, *multiply*, and *product*.

Materials

Program Materials

- Vocabulary Card 30 (product)
- Number 1–6 Cubes (optional) 
- Play Money 

Vocabulary

factor A number that is multiplied to get a product; for example: 3 (multiplier) $\times$ 5 (multiplicand) = 15 (product)

multiply To find the product of a number that is repeatedly added to itself ($4 + 4 + 4 = 3 \times 4 = 12$)

product The result of multiplying two or more numbers (factors)

1 Warm Up

Introduce each vocabulary word to students.
Say the word aloud.
Have students repeat the word.

After students have listened to the words, show them ***Vocabulary Card 30*** and have them repeat the word.

Write $2 \times 6 = 12$ on the board. Tell students that for this number sentence, they will multiply. Say *multiply*, and have students repeat the word. Write *multiply* on the board.

Point to the 12. Tell students that 12 is the product. Say *product*, and have students repeat the word. Write *product* on the board.

Point to the 2 and the 6. Tell students that 2 and 6 are called factors. Say *factor*, and have students repeat the word. Write *factor* on the board.

2 Engage

Distribute 12 of the same type of coin from the Play Money to each student.

- **How many coins do you have?** 12

Tell students to put their coins in 6 groups of 2.

- **How many coins do you have now?** 12

Write $2 + 2 + 2 + 2 + 2 + 2 = ?$ on the board.

- **What is the answer?** 12
- **How many times did I write a two?** 6

Write $2 \times 6 = ?$ on the board.

- **What is the product?** 12
- **What are the factors?** 2 and 6

Have students rearrange their coins into 3 groups of 4. Repeat the activity for this arrangement.

Organize students into pairs. Have them discover the factors for the product 24. Observe students, and encourage them to use the new vocabulary words in complete sentences.

Teacher's Note

Praise any attempts to use vocabulary taught during this program. Praise reinforces learning and makes uncomfortable situations easier for language learners.

Progress Monitoring

If . . .	Then . . .
If . . . students struggle to understand the activity,	**Then . . .** demonstrate by rearranging coins into additional factor groups.

3 Reflect

Extended Response

- **If each student has two pencils, how many pencils does the class have all together?**
- **Would you rather have (5 + 4) dollars or (5 × 4) dollars? Why?**
- **How can we use factors and products every day?**

Encourage student discussion of these questions and answers.

Progress Monitoring

If . . . students could use extra speaking practice,	**Then . . .** have them roll two Number 1–6 Cubes and say a sentence using the two numbers that come up; for example, *The factors are 2 and 4, and the product is 8.*

4 Assess

Informal Assessment

Have students complete the activity below to make sure they understand the vocabulary. As students use each word:

1. Check understanding.
2. Correct errors.
3. Recheck for understanding.

- Have students model 4 × 6 using coins.
- Have students say aloud the multiplication sentence and identify the factors and the product.

For each word, use the following rubric to assign a score.

The student can repeat the word when prompted. (1 point)

The student knows the word but does not know its meaning. (2 points)

The student has a vague idea of the word's meaning. (3 points)

The student knows the word and can use the word in context. (4 points)

Objective

Students can understand the meanings of the terms *dividend, divisor, quotient,* and *remainder.*

Materials

Program Materials

- Vocabulary Card 33 (quotient)
- Divide and Conquer, p. 124
- Two-Color Counters

Vocabulary

dividend The number that is to be divided
divisor The number that divides the dividend
quotient The answer to a division problem
remainder The number that is left over after dividing

1 Warm Up

Introduce each vocabulary word to students.
Say the word aloud.
Have students repeat the word.

Show students ***Vocabulary Card 33.***

Write $12 \times 3 = 36$ on the board.

- **What are the factors?** 12 and 3

Erase 12.

- **What number is missing?** 12

Below the original equation, write $36 \div 3 = ?$ Students should know the answer to this problem, because it is related to the multiplication problem; it is just written in a different way. Explain that 36 is the number that is divided and is called the dividend. Say *dividend,* and have students repeat the word. Write *dividend* on the board.

Point to the 3, and tell students the number that divides the dividend is called the divisor. Say *divisor,* and have students repeat the word. Write *divisor* on the board.

- **What is the answer?** 12

Tell students the answer to a division problem is called the *quotient.* Say *quotient,* and have students repeat the word. Write *quotient* on the board.

Repeat the activity with different dividends.

2 Engage

Organize students into groups of three or four. Distribute 24 Counters to each group. Have students work together to think of division problems to model with their Counters. Monitor groups to make sure students are using the new vocabulary words *dividend, divisor,* and *quotient* as they discuss the exercise.

Distribute 7 more Counters to each group. Then tell students to make 2 equal groups with the Counters. Let them know they may have some Counters left over.

- **How many Counters are in each equal group?** fifteen
- **Do you have any Counters left over? How many?** yes; one

Tell students that the one left-over Counter is called the remainder. Say *remainder,* and have students repeat the word. Write *remainder* on the board.

Elicit from students what they should call the quotient. If no one knows, tell them that this quotient should be read 15 *remainder* 1. Have students repeat until they are comfortable with saying the quotient with a remainder. Write 15 *remainder* 1 on the board. Tell students that we use the symbol *R* for the word *remainder* when we write. Erase *remainder,* and replace with R.

Organize students into pairs. Distribute a copy of Divide and Conquer, p. 124, to each student. Have students complete the worksheet. Then have students review their answers with their partners. Encourage them to discuss reasons for disagreement.

Teacher's Note

Tell students that it is okay to disagree with each other. It can help them learn if they have partners who are encouraging but offer suggestions for improvements.

Using Student Worksheets

After students complete the activity, help them complete the appropriate Practice for their levels of English development.

Level 1, Practice 1, p. 32

Level 2, Practice 2, p. 33

Level 3, Practice 3, p. 34

Chapter 4

Name ______________________ Date ____________

Practice 2

Look at the problems. Answer each question. Write your answers in complete sentences. Be ready to share your answers with the class.

$286 \div 4 = 71$ R 2

1. Which number is the divisor?

____

2. Which number is the dividend?

____

3. Which number is the remainder?

____

4. What is the quotient?

____

$247 \times 3 = 741$

5. What is the product?

____

6. What are the factors?

____

7. How many digits are in the product?

____

8. How many digits are in each factor?

____

Chapter 4

Name ______________________ Date ______________

Practice 3

Look at the examples, and follow the directions carefully.

29 × 3 = 87   **581 ÷ 29 = 20 R 1**

1. Circle the product.

2. Draw a triangle around the divisor.

3. Draw a box around the quotient.

4. Draw a star next to the remainder.

5. Write the factors on the lines.

   ______ ______

6. Underline all digits in the ones place.

Name ______________________ Date ____________

Unit 1 Final Assessment

Look at the division sentence. Determine if each sentence is true. Write *yes* or *no* on the blank.

85 ÷ 5 = 17

1. The dividend is 85. _____

2. The quotient has a remainder. _____

Answer each question.

3. **4,378** What number is in the tens place? _____

4. **5,788** How many digits are in this number? _____

5. What is the product of 600 × 6? _____

6. What number is left over? 633 ÷ 4 = 158 R 1 _____

Rational Numbers

Unit at a Glance

In this unit, students will learn the vocabulary associated with ***Number Worlds,*** Algebra Readiness, Rational Numbers. In this unit, students will identify and compare fractional and decimal parts of a whole, recognize prime and composite numbers and determine prime numbers to 50, write numbers as the product of their prime factors by using exponents to show multiples of a factor, and work with equivalent fractions and understand how they relate to percents. Before beginning the unit, assess students' general knowledge of math and vocabulary using the Individual Oral Assessment on page 37.

How Students Learn Vocabulary

Using visuals and manipulatives creates familiarity for English learners and has an immediate impact on learning language. For this unit, it will be helpful to have balance scales, math-link cubes, base-ten blocks, and Counters on hand so students can visualize the reality of the operations they will be conducting.

Some of the mathematical concepts practiced in this unit may be familiar to English learners, even though the vocabulary is not. Using the context of mathematics may actually be quite helpful for teaching new vocabulary. Offering students numerous opportunities to use new vocabulary will increase their ability to use the language quickly.

Academic Vocabulary Taught in Unit 2

Chapter 5	Chapter 6	Chapter 7	Chapter 8
decimal A number containing a decimal point **decimal number** A number that falls between two whole numbers **decimal point** A dot used to separate the ones digit from the tenths digit **denominator** The bottom number of a fraction; it shows the number of parts in the whole **fraction** A quantity expressing the division of one number by a second number, written as two numerals separated by a line **numerator** The top number of a fraction; it shows the number of equal parts	**integer** Any positive or negative whole number or zero **mixed number** A number consisting of a whole number and a fraction **negative number** A number that is less than zero **positive number** A number that is greater than zero	**exponent** A numeral or symbol placed at the upper right side of another numeral or symbol to indicate the number of times it is to be multiplied by itself **prime number** A whole number that has only two factors—the number itself and 1	**equivalent fractions** Fractions that name the same rational number **percent** A special fraction with a denominator of 100

Unit 2 Individual Oral Assessment

Directions: Read each question to the student, and record his or her oral responses. Some questions have teacher directions. Teacher directions are indicated in italics. Allow students to use pencil and paper to work their responses.

1. Is this an **integer**? *Show student the number 4.* **yes**
2. Is this a **fraction**? *Show student the number 5.75.* **no**
3. Where is the **decimal point**? *Show student the number 5.75.* **Student should point to the decimal point.**
4. Is this a **prime number**? *Write* 21 *on a piece of paper.* **no**
5. Which number is the **exponent**? *Write* 5^3 *on a piece of paper.* **3**
6. Which number is the **denominator**? *Write* $\frac{4}{5}$ *on a piece of paper.* **5**
7. Which of these is a **mixed number**? *Write* $\frac{1}{3}$, $\frac{4}{3}$, *and* $1\frac{1}{3}$ *on a piece of paper.* **$1\frac{1}{3}$**
8. Where is **negative** eight? *Show student a number line.* **Student should point to negative eight.**
9. What does 2^4 equal? Which number is the **exponent?** **16; 4**
10. Which of these is not a **prime number**? *Write* 3, 5, 7, 9 *on a piece of paper.* **9**
11. What is an **equivalent fraction** to 25%? **Accept any fraction equivalent to $\frac{1}{4}$.**
12. Tell me three **prime numbers.** **Student should say any three prime numbers.**
13. What **decimal** is equivalent to $\frac{2}{5}$? **0.40, or 0.4**

- **Beginning English Learners:** 0–3 of questions 1–10 correct
- **Intermediate English Learners:** 4–7 of questions 1–10 correct
- **Advanced English Learners:** 8–10 of questions 1–10 correct
- If the student is able to answer Questions 11–13, then he or she can understand the mathematics taught in this unit, but may still have difficulty with the academic vocabulary.

Use the Student Assessment Record, page 144, to record the assessment results.

Objective

Students can understand the meanings of the terms *fraction, numerator, denominator, decimal, decimal number,* and *decimal point.*

Materials

Program Materials

- Vocabulary Cards 6 (decimal) and 12 (fraction)
- Fractions and Decimals, p. 125
- Play Money 
- Fraction Tiles (optional) 

Additional Materials

Base-ten blocks 

Vocabulary

decimal A number containing a decimal point
decimal number A number that falls between two whole numbers
decimal point A dot used to separate the ones digit from the tenths digit
denominator The bottom number of a fraction; it shows the number of parts in the whole
fraction A quantity expressing the division of one number by a second number, written as two numerals separated by a line
numerator The top number of a fraction; it shows the number of equal parts

1 Warm Up

Introduce each vocabulary word to students.
Say the word aloud.
Have students repeat the word.

After students have had some practice listening to the words, show them ***Vocabulary Cards 6*** and **12.**

Review the names and values of coins. Distribute a handful of coins to each student, and have students create combinations with the coins. Ask students to tell the class how much they have altogether. As students tell the class their amounts, have the group practice expressing the values.

Tell students to find a combination for $1.45.

- **What coins did you use to make one dollar and forty-five cents?** Possible answer: five quarters and two dimes

Write 1.45 on the board.

- **Is this a whole number?** no
- **Is this amount more than or less than one?** more than
- **Is this amount more than or less than two?** less than

Tell students that when a number is between two whole numbers, it is called a decimal number. Say *decimal,* and have students repeat the word. Write *decimal* on the board.

Point to the decimal point. Ask if anyone knows what it is called. Say *decimal point,* and have students repeat the term. Write *decimal point* on the board.

2 Engage

Hold up the 1,000 cube of the base-ten blocks set.

- **How many cubes am I holding?** 1

Pull apart the cube so it is in halves.

- **What did I do to the cube?** broke it in half

Write $\frac{1}{2}$ on the board. Review the vocabulary word *fraction.* Say the word, and have students repeat the word. Write *fraction* on the board.

Point to the denominator. Review the denominator as the number in a fraction that shows how many parts are in the whole. Show students how the two halves of the cube are combined to make a whole piece. Say *denominator,* and have students repeat the word. Write *denominator* on the board.

- **What is the denominator in this fraction?** 2
- **What does it show us?** the number of parts in the whole

Point to the numerator. Review the numerator as the number in a fraction that shows the number of equal parts. Show students one of the halves of the cube, and reiterate that this is one-half. Say *numerator,* and have students repeat the word. Write *numerator* on the board.

- **What is the numerator in this fraction?** 1
- **What does it show us?** the number of equal parts

Repeat the activity to show $\frac{1}{5}$, $\frac{2}{5}$, and so on until students are comfortable with the vocabulary.

Write the number 8.153 on the board. Ask students to tell you what they know about this number. Show them that another way to write this number is $8\frac{153}{1{,}000}$. Repeat for other equivalent fractions and decimals.

Organize students into pairs. Distribute a copy of Fractions and Decimals, p. 125, to each student. Have partners complete the worksheet. Have students conduct a peer review of the worksheet with another pair of students as you monitor them.

Teacher's Note

English learners may already understand the mathematical concepts being taught but lack the English vocabulary to express them. Use students' understanding of the concepts to your advantage when introducing words.

Progress Monitoring

If . . .	Then . . .
If . . . students are doing well with this activity,	**Then . . .** organize students into pairs and distribute a set of Fraction Tiles to each pair of students. Give partners time to explore the Fraction Tiles and describe what they discover.

3 Reflect

Extended Response

- **How do we use fractions every day?**
- **If Gigi answers 8 out of 12 questions correctly, did she correctly answer $\frac{2}{3}$ of the questions? How do you know?**
- **Can you draw a picture to show a fraction? If so, how?**
- **How are decimals similar to fractions?**
- **Which is easier to understand, fractions or decimals?**

Encourage student discussion of these questions and answers.

Progress Monitoring

If . . .	Then . . .
If . . . some students struggle with the lesson vocabulary,	**Then . . .** work with them individually or as a small group.

4 Assess

Informal Assessment

Have students complete the activity below to make sure they understand the vocabulary. As students use each word:

1. Check understanding.
2. Correct errors.
3. Recheck for understanding.

Write $\frac{3}{4}$ and 0.75 on the board. Have students identify the fraction, the decimal, the numerator, the denominator, and the decimal point.

For each word, use the following rubric to assign a score.

The student can repeat the word when prompted. (1 point)

The student knows the word but does not know its meaning. (2 points)

The student has a vague idea of the word's meaning. (3 points)

The student knows the word and can use the word in context. (4 points)

Chapter 6

Unit 2 • Rational Numbers

Objective

Students can understand the meanings of the terms *mixed number, integer, positive number,* and *negative number.*

Materials

Program Materials

- Vocabulary Cards 15 (integer), 20 (mixed number), and 21 (negative number)
- Magnetic Number Lines 
- Fraction Tiles 

Vocabulary

integer Any positive or negative whole number or zero
mixed number A number consisting of a whole number and a fraction
negative number A number that is less than zero
positive number A number that is greater than zero

1 Warm Up

Introduce each vocabulary word.
Say the word aloud.
Have students repeat the word.

After students have had some experience listening to the words, show students ***Vocabulary Cards 15, 20,*** and ***21,*** and say each word.

Review fraction and decimal vocabulary. Say a number, such as *three and five tenths.* Have one volunteer write the number as a fraction on the board, and have another volunteer write the same number as a decimal. Repeat for several numbers.

Write $1\frac{1}{3}$ on the board.

- **Is this a fraction? Why or why not?** Accept reasonable answers.
- **What is different about it?** Students may point out that this number is made up of a whole number and a fraction.

Tell students that this number is made up of a whole number and a fraction and is called a mixed number. Say *mixed number,* and have students repeat the term. Write *mixed number* on the board.

2 Engage

Organize students into pairs. Distribute a Magnetic Number Line to each pair of students. Say *number line,* and have students repeat the term. Have students label the Magnetic Number Lines with 0 at the middle hatch mark, positive numbers extending to the right, and negative numbers extending to the left. Have students point to +6.

- **Is this a whole number or part of a number?** whole number

Tell students that whole numbers and zero are called integers. Say *integer,* and have students repeat the word. Write *integer* on the board.

Have students point to +6 again. Tell them that this number is 6 away from zero and it is 6 more than zero. Tell students it is a positive number. Say *positive number,* and have students repeat the term. Write *positive number* on the board.

Now have students point to −6.

- **Is this number 6 away from zero?** yes
- **Is this number 6 more than zero?** no

Tell students that this number is less than zero and is called a negative number. Say *negative number,* and have students repeat the term. Write *negative number* on the board.

Have students find +7 on the Magnetic Number Line.

- **Is this a whole number or part of a number?** whole number
- **Is this number an integer?** yes
- **Is this number positive or negative?** positive

Write $\frac{1}{2}$ on the board.

- **Is this a whole number or part of a number?** part of a number
- **Is this number an integer?** no

Continue checking concepts with other integers and non-integers until students seem comfortable with the vocabulary.

Teacher's Note

Concept checking is an important part of teaching to English learners. When introducing vocabulary, ask questions to determine whether students understand the meanings of words and ideas. Ask concept-check questions to individual students and occasionally to the whole group.

Progress Monitoring

If . . .	Then . . .
If . . . students understand the vocabulary but need more work with the concepts,	**Then . . .** have students use Fraction Tiles to create different fraction combinations, including mixed numbers. Have them practice the correct language to describe a mixed number.

3 Reflect

Extended Response

- **Why do we use negative numbers?**
- **Would you rather have a positive or negative amount in your bank account?**
- **How is two dollars and twenty-five cents like a mixed number? Can you write it as a mixed number?**
- **How are negative numbers different from positive numbers?**
- **How are negative numbers the same as positive numbers?**

Encourage student discussion of these questions and answers.

Progress Monitoring

If . . .	Then . . .
If . . . students need practice with the lesson vocabulary,	**Then . . .** challenge them to quiz each other by writing positive and negative integers on index cards. Have students work in pairs to discuss as much about the number as they can; for example, *It is a negative integer,* or *It is not an integer.* Students should plot the integers on a number line.

4 Assess

Informal Assessment

Have students complete the activity below to make sure they understand the vocabulary. As students use each word:

1. Check understanding.
2. Correct errors.
3. Recheck for understanding.

- Show students a set of integers, fractions, and decimal numbers. Have students identify the integers.
- Show students a set of random integers. Have them identify each integer as positive or negative.

For each word, use the following rubric to assign a score.

The student can repeat the word when prompted. (1 point)

The student knows the word but does not know its meaning. (2 points)

The student has a vague idea of the word's meaning. (3 points)

The student knows the word and can use the word in context. (4 points)

Objective

Students can understand the meanings of the terms *exponent* and *prime number.*

Materials

Program Materials

- Vocabulary Cards 11 (exponent) and 28 (prime number)
- Number Cards (0–9), ***Teacher Edition,*** p. B2

Vocabulary

exponent A numeral or symbol placed at the upper right side of another numeral or symbol to indicate the number of times it is to be multiplied by itself

prime number A whole number that has only two factors—the number itself and 1

1 Warm Up

Introduce each vocabulary word to students.
Say the word aloud.
Have students repeat the word.

After students have had some practice listening to the words, show them ***Vocabulary Cards* 11** and **28.**

Play a quick multiplication game. Make four copies of Number Cards (0–9), ***Teacher Edition,*** p. B2. Cut out the cards, shuffle them, and randomly draw two cards. Hold them up for students to see. Have students give a multiplication sentence for each pair of cards; for example, *four times six equals twenty-four.*

2 Engage

Write $4 \times 6 = 24$ on the board. Point to 4×6.

- **What do we call numbers that are multiplied together?** factors

Tell students that factors are numbers that are multiplied together to find a product. Say *factors,* and have students repeat the word. Write *factors* on the board.

- **Is 4 a factor of 12?** yes
- **Is 6 a factor of 8?** no
- **Are 4 and 6 factors of 24?** yes

Draw the first branches of a factor tree for the number 24 on the board.

- **When determining sets of factors for the branches, do not use the number itself or 1.**
- **What are the factors of the number 4?** 2 and 2
- **What are the factors of the number 6?** 2 and 3

Write the next branch of the factor tree.

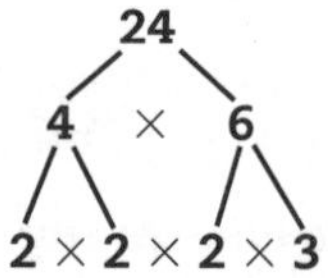

- **What are the factors of the number 2?** 1 and 2
- **What are the factors of the number 3?** 1 and 3

Tell students that numbers whose only factors are 1 and itself are called prime numbers. Say *prime number,* and have students repeat the term. Write *prime number* on the board.

Explain that an easier way to write $2 \times 2 \times 2 \times 3$ is $2^3 \times 3$. The 2 is the base, or the factor. The 3 is the exponent, or the number of times the factor is multiplied by itself. Say *exponent,* and have students repeat the word. Write *exponent* on the board.

Teacher's Note

Explain to students that exponential notation makes it easier to work with large numbers. Exponents are sometimes called "powers." Numbers such as 10, 100, and 1,000 are called "powers of 10" because these numbers can be written as 10 with an exponent.

Progress Monitoring

If . . .	Then . . .
students need additional practice with factors and prime numbers,	provide another example of a factor tree for the number 24 using the factors 8 and 3. Have students create their own factor trees with a partner.

3 Reflect

Extended Response

- **What is a prime number?**
- **Why are exponents useful?**
- **What is one reason why exponents might be used?**
- **What jobs might require you to use exponents?**

Encourage student discussion of these questions and answers.

Progress Monitoring

If . . .	Then . . .
If . . . a student hesitates to contribute to the class discussion voluntarily,	**Then . . .** ask that student a direct question that you know he or she can answer easily.

4 Assess

Informal Assessment

Have students complete each activity below to make sure they understand the vocabulary. As students use each word:

1. Check understanding.
2. Correct errors.
3. Recheck for understanding.

- Write 5^3 on the board. Have students identify the exponent.
- Have students define *prime number* and identify three prime numbers.

For each word, use the following rubric to assign a score.

The student can repeat the word when prompted. (1 point)

The student knows the word but does not know its meaning. (2 points)

The student has a vague idea of the word's meaning. (3 points)

The student knows the word and can use the word in context. (4 points)

Objective

Students can understand the meanings of the terms *equivalent fractions* and *percent.*

Materials

Program Materials

- Vocabulary Cards 10 (equivalent fractions) and 25 (percent)
- Percents and Their Equivalents, p. 126
- 10 × 10 Grid, *Teacher Edition,* p. B13
- Two-Color Counters (optional)

Additional Materials

Colored pencils

Vocabulary

equivalent fractions Fractions that name the same rational number

percent A special fraction with a denominator of 100

1 Warm Up

Introduce each vocabulary word to students.
Say the word aloud.
Have students repeat the word.

After students listen to the words, show them ***Vocabulary Cards* 10** and **25.**

Have students fold a piece of paper in half and then open up the paper. Ask students to color one half of the paper.

- **How much did you color?** $\frac{1}{2}$

Write $\frac{1}{2}$ on the board.

Have students fold their papers in half along the same fold, and then fold them in half again.

- **How many total parts are there?** 4
- **How many parts are colored?** 2

Next to the fraction $\frac{1}{2}$, write $\frac{2}{4}$.

- **Are these the same fractions?** no
- **Do they represent equal amounts?** yes

Repeat for $\frac{4}{8}$ and $\frac{8}{16}$, if necessary. Tell students that these fractions represent the same amounts and are called equivalent fractions. Say *equivalent fractions,* and have students repeat the term. Write *equivalent fractions* on the board.

2 Engage

Distribute a copy of 10 × 10 Grid, ***Teacher Edition,*** p. B13, to each student.

- **How many squares are on this grid?** 100

Tell students that the total amount on this grid is one hundred. Percent can be expressed as parts per hundred. All of the squares together can be represented by the fraction $\frac{100}{100}$, which is equal to one hundred parts per hundred, or 100 percent. Say *percent*, and have students repeat the word. Write *percent* on the board.

Have students use Counters or pencil marks to represent the fraction $\frac{10}{100}$ on the 10 × 10 grid.

- **How many squares did you mark out of 100 total squares?** 10 out of 100
- **What percent of 100 is that?** 10%
- **If you want to show 25 percent, how many squares should you mark?** 25 squares

Show students how 25% can be written as the fraction $\frac{25}{100}$.

- **Is this an equivalent fraction to 25%?** yes
- **What is the decimal equivalent to 25%, or $\frac{25}{100}$?** 0.25
- **What is an equivalent fraction to 50%?** $\frac{50}{100}$, or $\frac{1}{2}$
- **What is the decimal equivalent to 50%?** 0.50, or 0.5

Distribute a copy of Percents and Their Equivalents, p. 126, to each student. Organize students into pairs. Have partners work together to complete the worksheet. Have pairs orally conduct a peer review of the work with other pairs as you monitor.

Teacher's Note

When you work with percents, it is sometimes useful to write them in decimal form. To replace a percent with an equivalent decimal, divide the percent by 100. Start with the percent, and move the decimal point two digits to the left.

Chapter 8

Name ______________________ Date ____________

Practice 2

Ask your classmates the following questions. Have a different person answer each question. Write your answers in complete sentences. Be ready to share your answers with the class.

1. Who knows what an integer is? What is an integer?

____

____

2. Who can point to a negative number? What is a negative number?

____

3. Who can write the number 32 using an exponent? What is the base, or factor, and what is the exponent? What is an exponent? ______________________________

____

____

____

4. Who can say the prime numbers to 50? What is a prime number?

____

____

____

5. Who knows an equivalent fraction to $\frac{4}{6}$? What is an equivalent fraction?

____

____

____

6. Who knows a percent that equals $\frac{8}{10}$? What is a percent?

____

____

Chapter 8

Name ______________________ Date ____________

Practice 3

Follow the directions.

1. Write $2 \times 2 \times 2 \times 2$ as a base and an exponent. ____________

2. Write $\frac{1}{4} + \frac{3}{4} + \frac{1}{4}$ as a mixed number. ____________

3. Circle the equivalent fraction to 20%.

   0.20 $\frac{4}{5}$ $\frac{2}{5}$ $\frac{1}{5}$

4. $\frac{6}{7}$ Draw a box around the numerator. ____________________________

5. Write the equivalent decimal to $\frac{4}{5}$. ____________

6. What are negative numbers? Write your answer in a complete sentence.

   ____

Chapter 8

Name ______________________ Date ____________

Unit 2 Final Assessment

Determine if each sentence is true. **Write** *yes* or *no* on the blank.

1. The fraction $\frac{3}{5}$ is equivalent to 60%. ________

2. 4^3 equals $3 \times 3 \times 3 \times 3$. ________

Look at the numbers. **Write** the answer to each question.

3. $\frac{2}{3}$ Is the number 2 a numerator or a denominator? ____________

4. **23** Is the number prime or negative? ________

Complete the table.

	Fraction	Decimal	Percent
5	$\frac{2}{4}$		
6		0.875	

Operations on Rational Numbers

Unit at a Glance

In this unit, students will learn the vocabulary associated with ***Number Worlds,*** Algebra Readiness, Operations on Rational Numbers. In this unit, students will learn to add, subtract, multiply, and divide integers, fractions, and decimals; take positive numbers to whole-number powers; convert among fractions, decimals, and percents; use proportions; and work with inverses. Before beginning the unit, assess students' general knowledge of math and vocabulary using the Individual Oral Assessment on page 51.

How Students Learn Vocabulary

Using visuals and manipulatives creates familiarity for English learners and has an immediate impact on learning language. For this unit, it will be helpful to have Fraction Tiles, base-ten blocks, and math-link cubes on hand so students can visualize the reality of the operations they will be conducting.

Concept checking is also an important part of teaching to English learners. When introducing vocabulary, ask questions to determine whether students understand the meanings of words and ideas. Ask concept-check questions to individual students and occasionally to the whole group.

Academic Vocabulary Taught in Unit 3

Chapter 9	Chapter 10	Chapter 11	Chapter 12
addend Any number or quantity that is to be added to another **addition** The process of adding two or more numbers together **ratio** The comparison of two numbers by division **sum** The answer to an addition problem	**product** The result of multiplying two or more numbers (factors) **quotient** The answer to a division problem **rational number** A number that can be expressed as a quotient of two integers or as an integer	**denominator** The bottom number of a fraction; it shows the number of parts in the whole **equal** Identical in value or notation **numerator** The top number of a fraction; it shows the number of equal parts	**inverse** A number that when added to or multiplied by the original number results in the identity element for that operation **reciprocal** One of two quantities whose product is 1; for example, $\frac{3}{4}$ and $\frac{4}{3}$ are reciprocals of each other

Unit 3 Individual Oral Assessment

Directions: Read each question to the student, and record his or her oral responses. Some questions have teacher directions. Teacher directions are indicated in italics. Allow students to use pencil and paper to work their responses.

1. Is this the **sum**? *Write* $4 + 5 = 9$ *on a piece of paper. Point to the 4.* **no**

2. Is this an **addend**? *Write* $8 = 2 + 6$ *on a piece of paper. Point to the 6.* **yes**

3. Is this a **product**? *Write* $6 \times 7 = 42$ *on a piece of paper. Point to 42.* **yes**

4. Is this a **ratio**? *Write* $\frac{6}{7}$ *on a piece of paper.* **yes**

5. Which number is the **denominator**? *Show student the same fraction.* **7**

6. Are these **rational numbers**? *Write* $\frac{2}{4}$ *and 2 on a piece of paper.* **yes**

7. Are these numbers **equal**? *Write* 30% *and* $\frac{3}{10}$ *on a piece of paper.* **yes**

8. What is the **product** of 4 and 9? **36**

9. What is the additive **inverse** of –8? **8 or positive 8**

10. Which number is the **numerator**? *Write* $\frac{2}{4}$ *on a piece of paper.* **2**

11. What is the multiplicative **inverse** of $-\frac{3}{5}$? $-\frac{5}{3}$

12. What is the **reciprocal** of $\frac{7}{8}$? $\frac{8}{7}$

13. What percent is **equal** to $\frac{3}{4}$? **75%**

- **Beginning English Learners:** 0–3 of Questions 1–10 correct
- **Intermediate English Learners:** 4–7 of Questions 1–10 correct
- **Advanced English Learners:** 8–10 of Questions 1–10 correct
- If the student is able to answer Questions 11–13, then he or she can understand the mathematics taught in this unit, but may still have difficulty with the academic vocabulary.

Use the Student Assessment Record, page 144, to record the assessment results.

9

Objective

Students can understand the meanings of the terms *ratio, addition, addend,* and *sum.*

Materials

Program Materials

- Vocabulary Card 36 (ratio)
- Addition Vocabulary and Ratios, p. 127

Vocabulary

addend Any number or quantity that is to be added to another
addition The process of adding two or more numbers together
ratio The comparison of two numbers by division
sum The answer to an addition problem

1 Warm Up

Introduce each vocabulary word to students.
Say the word aloud.
Have students repeat the word.

After students have listened to the words, show them ***Vocabulary Card 36*** and have them repeat the word.

Review the terms *percent* and *equivalent* with students.

- **If I have 8 books, and I give 50% of them away, how many do I have left?** 4
- **What is an equivalent fraction to 50%?** $\frac{50}{100}$ or $\frac{1}{2}$
- **What is an equivalent decimal to 50%?** 0.50, or 0.5
- **What does *percent* mean?** for each one hundred
- **What does *per* mean?** for each

2 Engage

- **What is another way to say *one paper for each student?*** one paper per student
- **One paper per how many students?** one

Write $\frac{1}{1}$ on the board.

- **What is another way to say *one paper for every two students?*** one paper per two students
- **One paper per how many students?** 2

Write $\frac{1}{2}$ on the board.

Tell students that you have just discovered a ratio. Ratios can be written as fractions such as $\frac{1}{2}$ (*one out of two* or *one for every two*) or as 1:2 (*one to two*). Say *ratio*, and have students repeat the term. Write *ratio* on the board.

Organize students into pairs. Have each pair of students determine ratios for different events or circumstances such as the number of eggs per carton, the number of days per week, and so on.

Write 100 + 200 = *?* on the board.

Tell students that the process of adding two numbers together is called addition. Say *addition*, and have students repeat the word. Write *addition* on the board.

Point to 100. Tell students that a number that is added to another number is called an addend. Say *addend*, and have students repeat the word. Write *addend* on the board.

- **What is the answer?** 300

Write the answer on the board.

- **Is this an addend?** no

Tell students that the answer to an addition problem is called the sum. Say *sum*, and have students repeat the word. Write *sum* on the board.

Distribute a copy of Addition Vocabulary and Ratios, p. 127, to each student. Have students work with a partner to complete the worksheet. Review the worksheet as a class.

Teacher's Note

When you conduct a partner activity but have an odd number of students, have one student act as "teacher" and observe partners and give feedback.

Progress Monitoring

If . . .	Then . . .
If . . . students master the lesson vocabulary,	**Then . . .** have students brainstorm a list of rates, and write the ratios for each.

3 Reflect

Extended Response

- **How can we use a ratio to show how many boy students are in the class?**
- **There are 20 students in the class, and 9 students are girls. What does the ratio 9:11 mean?**
- **Using the above example, what does the ratio $\frac{9}{20}$ mean?**
- **Suppose a school's student-to-teacher ratio is 22 to 1. What does that mean?**
- **Which is better, a student-to-teacher ratio of 22 to 1, or a student-to-teacher ratio of 12 to 1? Explain.**

Encourage student discussion of these questions and answers.

Progress Monitoring

If . . .	Then . . .
If . . . students are not confident with their responses,	**Then . . .** encourage them by praising them for each attempt to use English and the lesson vocabulary.

4 Assess

Informal Assessment

Have students complete the activity below to make sure they understand the vocabulary. As students use each word:

1. Check understanding.
2. Correct errors.
3. Recheck for understanding.

- Have students give an example of a ratio and explain how ratios can be used in the real world.
- Write $635 = 522 + 113$ on the board. Have students identify the addends and the sum.

For each word, use the following rubric to assign a score.

The student can repeat the word when prompted. (1 point)

The student knows the word but does not know its meaning. (2 points)

The student has a vague idea of the word's meaning. (3 points)

The student knows the word and can use the word in context. (4 points)

10 ers

Objective

Students can review the meanings of the terms *quotient* and *product* and can understand the meaning of the term *rational number.*

Materials

Program Materials

- Vocabulary Cards 30 (product) and 33 (quotient)
- Fraction Tiles 

Additional Materials

- Math-link cubes 
- Base-ten blocks 

Vocabulary

product The result of multiplying two or more numbers (factors)
quotient The answer to a division problem
rational number A number that can be expressed as a quotient of two integers or as an integer

1 Warm Up

Introduce each vocabulary word to students.
Say the word aloud.
Have students repeat the word.

Write $3 \times 4 = 12$ on the board.

■ **Is this multiplication or division?** multiplication

Point to the 12.

■ **What is this called?** product

Say *product*, and have students repeat the word. Write *product* on the board.

Write $12 \div 4 = 3$ on the board.

■ **Is this multiplication or division?** division

Point to the 3.

■ **What is this called?** quotient

Say *quotient*, and have students repeat the word. Write *quotient* on the board.

After students have listened to the words, show them ***Vocabulary Cards 30*** and **33,** and have them repeat the words.

2 Engage

Use base-ten blocks to show students how splitting the 1,000 cube in two equal pieces is like dividing one whole by two. Introduce the fraction as the quotient from the division sentence $1 \div 2 = \frac{1}{2}$.

■ **Is $\frac{1}{2}$ a ratio?** yes

Tell students that numbers written as a ratio, or the quotient of two integers, are called rational numbers. Say *rational number*, and have students repeat the term. Write *rational number* on the board.

Write $\frac{4}{5}$ on the board.

■ **Is this a rational number?** yes

Repeat for other fractions.

Write $12 \div 2 = 6$ on the board.

■ **Is this a rational number?**

Students may say *no* because the quotient is not a fraction. Show them how the number 6 can be written as a fraction, such as $\frac{6}{1}$, $\frac{12}{2}$, $\frac{18}{3}$ and so on. Integers are also rational numbers.

Organize students into pairs. Distribute math-link cubes, base-ten clocks, or Fraction Tiles to each pair of students. Have students experiment with fractions as quotients. Encourage students to try dividing a number larger than one; for example, three wholes divided by six equals $\frac{3}{6}$ or $\frac{1}{2}$.

Teacher's Note

Praise any attempts to use vocabulary taught during this program. Praise reinforces learning and makes uncomfortable situations easier for language learners.

Progress Monitoring

If . . . students have mastered the vocabulary and the content of this activity,

Then . . . give each pair of students a set of Fraction Tiles and have students work backward to determine products and quotients represented by the set of tiles.

3 Reflect

Extended Response

- **How is the fraction $\frac{14}{2}$ like the division problem $14 \div 2$?**
- **If each student has one sister, how many sisters do we have all together? Is the answer a product or a quotient?**
- **Imagine that you need to read 3 books in 75 minutes. Can you think of a rational number to show this? Is the answer a product or a quotient?**
- **How might we use factors and products every day?**

Encourage student discussion of these questions and answers.

Progress Monitoring

If . . .	Then . . .
If . . . some students struggle with the lesson vocabulary,	**Then . . .** work with them individually or as a small group.

4 Assess

Informal Assessment

Have students complete the activity below to make sure they understand the vocabulary. As students use each word:

1. Check understanding.
2. Correct errors.
3. Recheck for understanding.

- Have students define *rational number* in their own words.
- Write a multiplication problem and a division problem on the board. Have students identify the product and the quotient.

For each word, use the following rubric to assign a score.

The student can repeat the word when prompted. (1 point)

The student knows the word but does not know its meaning. (2 points)

The student has a vague idea of the word's meaning. (3 points)

The student knows the word and can use the word in context. (4 points)

Chapter 11

Unit 3 • Operations on Rational Numbers

Objective

Students can understand the meanings of the terms *numerator*, *denominator*, and *equal*.

Materials

Program Materials

- Fraction Tiles 

Additional Materials

- Base-ten blocks 
- Math-link cubes 

Vocabulary

denominator The bottom number of a fraction; it shows the number of parts in the whole
equal Identical in value or notation
numerator The top number of a fraction; it shows the number of equal parts

1 Warm Up

Write the fraction $\frac{1}{2}$ on the board. Point to the fraction and each of its parts as you introduce the vocabulary.

Introduce each vocabulary word to students.
Say the word aloud.
Have students repeat the word.
Write each word on the board.

Hold up the 1,000 cube of the base-ten blocks set.

- **How many cubes am I holding?** 1
- **Is it a whole piece or part of a piece?** a whole piece

Pull apart the cube so it is in halves.

- **What did I do to the cube?** broke it in half

Write $\frac{1}{2}$ on the board. Say *fraction*, and have students repeat the word. Write *fraction* on the board.

2 Engage

Point to the denominator. Review the denominator as the number in a fraction that shows how many parts are in the whole. Show students how the halves of the cube are combined to make a whole piece. Say *denominator*, and have students repeat the word. Write *denominator* on the board.

- **What is the denominator in this fraction?** 2
- **What does it tell us?** the number of parts in the whole

Point to the numerator. Review the numerator as the number in a fraction that shows the number of equal parts. Show students one of the halves of the cube, and reiterate that this is one-half. Say *numerator*, and have students repeat the word. Write *numerator* on the board.

- **What is the numerator in this fraction?** 1
- **What does it tell us?** the number of equal parts

Repeat the activity to show $\frac{1}{5}$, $\frac{2}{5}$, and so on until students are comfortable with the vocabulary.

Use Fraction Tiles to show students representations of $\frac{2}{8}$ and $\frac{1}{4}$. Write $\frac{2}{8}$ and $\frac{1}{4}$ on the board.

- **Are these the same?** yes

Tell students that even though fractions may be written differently, they may be equal. Say *equal*, and have students repeat the word. Write *equal* on the board. Introduce the idea that the two fractions you have written on the board are equivalent by reducing $\frac{2}{8}$ to $\frac{1}{4}$.

Organize students into pairs. Distribute a set of Fraction Tiles or math-link cubes to each pair of students. Have students create models of fractions and write five of their fractions on a piece of paper. Then have them trade papers with another pair. Each pair should identify the numerator and denominator, and then identify the fraction by its name. Praise students for practicing the new vocabulary.

Teacher's Note

Spanish-speaking students may recognize the vocabulary words *fraction, numerator*, and *denominator* as cognates. Confirm that these words have the same meanings in both languages.

Progress Monitoring

If . . .	Then . . .
If . . . students have mastered the vocabulary,	**Then . . .** give partners more time to explore the Fraction Tiles and describe what they discover.

3 Reflect

Extended Response

- **How do we use fractions every day?**
- **What does the denominator tell you? Why is it important?**
- **Can you draw a picture to show a fraction? How?**
- **Imagine that a sign at a store says *half off*. What does *half off* mean?**

Encourage student discussion of these questions and answers.

Progress Monitoring

If . . .	Then . . .
students hesitate to contribute to class discussions,	monitor those students closely as they interact with others in pairwork or small groups to make sure they are absorbing the instruction.

4 Assess

Informal Assessment

Have students complete the activity below to make sure they understand the vocabulary. As students use each word:

1. Check understanding.
2. Correct errors.
3. Recheck for understanding.

- Write a set of fractions on the board. Have students identify the numerator and denominator of each fraction.
- Have students determine if any of the fractions are equal.

For each word, use the following rubric to assign a score.

The student can repeat the word when prompted. (1 point)

The student knows the word but does not know its meaning. (2 points)

The student has a vague idea of the word's meaning. (3 points)

The student knows the word and can use the word in context. (4 points)

12

Objective

Students can understand the meanings of the terms *reciprocal* and *inverse.*

Materials

Program Materials

- Vocabulary Card 37 (reciprocal)
- Reciprocals and Inverses, p. 128
- Fraction Tiles 

Vocabulary

inverse A number that when added to or multiplied by the original number results in the identity element for that operation

reciprocal One of two quantities whose product is 1; for example, $\frac{3}{4}$ and $\frac{4}{3}$ are reciprocals of each other

1 Warm Up

Introduce each vocabulary word to students.
Say the word aloud.
Have students repeat the word.
Write each word on the board as you introduce it.

After students have listened to the words, show them *Vocabulary Card 37* and have them repeat the word.

Distribute Fraction Tiles to each student. Have students create equivalent fraction pairs, such as $\frac{2}{8}$ and $\frac{1}{4}$.

2 Engage

Review the fractions students created in the **Warm Up.**

Write $\frac{3}{4}$ on the board. Next to it, write $\frac{4}{3}$. Ask students what they notice about these numbers. Tell them that fractions are reciprocal if their product is 1 when they are multiplied. Say *reciprocal*, and have students repeat the word. Write *reciprocal* on the board.

- **What is the reciprocal of $\frac{2}{3}$?** $\frac{3}{2}$
- **What is the reciprocal of $\frac{8}{5}$?** $\frac{5}{8}$
- **What is the reciprocal of 2?** $\frac{1}{2}$

Write $\frac{4}{5} \times \frac{5}{4} = ?$ on the board.

- **What is the answer?** 1

If students need help determining the answer, show them that $\frac{4}{5} \times \frac{5}{4} = \frac{20}{20} = 1$.

Tell students that because the product is always 1 when reciprocals are multiplied, they are also called multiplicative inverses. Say *inverse*, and have students repeat the word. Write *inverse* on the board.

Write the word *multiplicative* on the board.

- **What other word does this word look like?** multiply or multiplication

Write $3 + -3 = ?$ on the board.

- **What is the answer?** 0

Tell students that when the sum is zero when two numbers are added together, the numbers are called additive inverses.

Write the word *additive* on the board.

- **What other word does this word look like?** add or addition
- **What is the additive inverse of –7?** 7
- **What is the multiplicative inverse of –7?** $-\frac{1}{7}$
- **What is the additive inverse of $\frac{5}{4}$?** $-\frac{5}{4}$
- **What is the multiplicative inverse of $\frac{5}{4}$?** $\frac{4}{5}$

Distribute a copy of Reciprocals and Inverses, p. 128, to each student. Organize students into pairs. Have students complete the worksheet with their partners. Review the worksheet as a class.

Teacher's Note

If students need visual references for additive inverses, try using a number line positioned vertically instead of horizontally.

Using Student Worksheets

After students complete the activity, help them complete the appropriate Practice for their levels of English development.

Level 1, Practice 1, p. 60

Level 2, Practice 2, p. 61

Level 3, Practice 3, p. 62

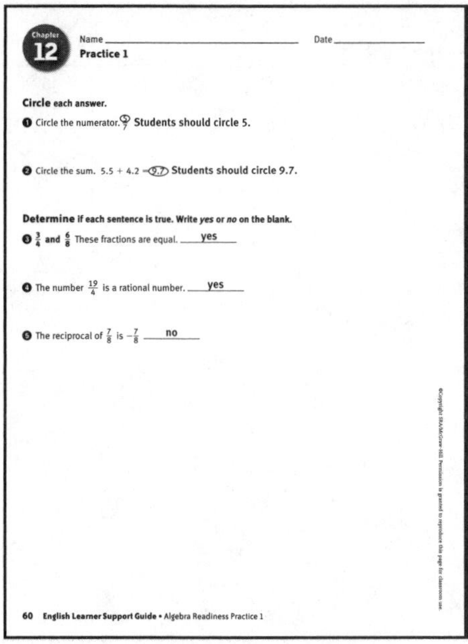

Chapter 12 Name ______ Date ______
Practice 1

Circle each answer.

1. Circle the numerator. $\frac{5}{7}$ **Students should circle 5.**
2. Circle the sum. 5.5 + 4.2 = 9.7 **Students should circle 9.7.**

Determine if each sentence is true. Write *yes* or *no* on the blank.

3. $\frac{3}{4}$ and $\frac{6}{8}$ These fractions are equal. __yes__
4. The number $\frac{19}{4}$ is a rational number. __yes__
5. The reciprocal of $\frac{7}{8}$ is $-\frac{7}{8}$ __no__

60 English Learner Support Guide • Algebra Readiness Practice 1

©Copyright SRA/McGraw-Hill. Permission is granted to reproduce this page for classroom use.

Practice 1, p.60

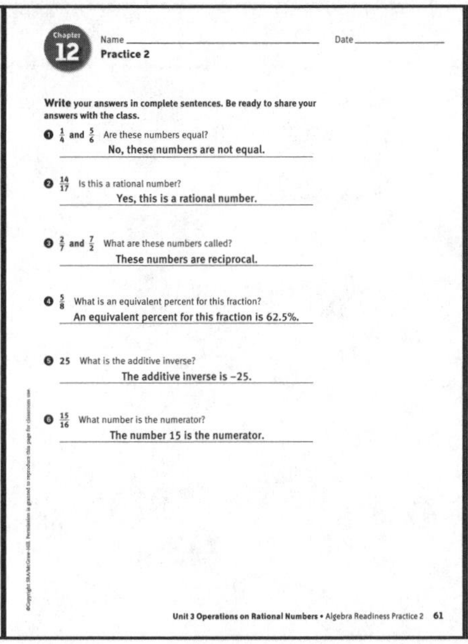

Chapter 12 Name ______ Date ______
Practice 2

Write your answers in complete sentences. Be ready to share your answers with the class.

1. $\frac{1}{4}$ and $\frac{5}{6}$ Are these numbers equal?
   No, these numbers are not equal.
2. $\frac{14}{17}$ Is this a rational number?
   Yes, this is a rational number.
3. $\frac{2}{7}$ and $\frac{7}{2}$ What are these numbers called?
   These numbers are reciprocal.
4. $\frac{5}{8}$ What is an equivalent percent for this fraction?
   An equivalent percent for this fraction is 62.5%.
5. 25 What is the additive inverse?
   The additive inverse is −25.
6. $\frac{15}{16}$ What number is the numerator?
   The number 15 is the numerator.

Unit 3 Operations on Rational Numbers • Algebra Readiness Practice 2 61

©Copyright SRA/McGraw-Hill. Permission is granted to reproduce this page for classroom use.

Practice 2, p.61

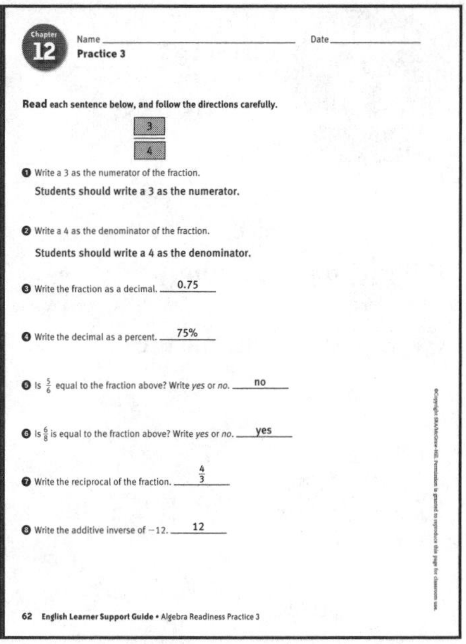

Chapter 12 Name ______ Date ______
Practice 3

Read each sentence below, and follow the directions carefully.

$\frac{3}{4}$

1. Write a 3 as the numerator of the fraction.
   Students should write a 3 as the numerator.
2. Write a 4 as the denominator of the fraction.
   Students should write a 4 as the denominator.
3. Write the fraction as a decimal. __0.75__
4. Write the decimal as a percent. __75%__
5. Is $\frac{5}{6}$ equal to the fraction above? Write *yes* or *no*. __no__
6. Is $\frac{6}{8}$ is equal to the fraction above? Write *yes* or *no*. __yes__
7. Write the reciprocal of the fraction. __$\frac{4}{3}$__
8. Write the additive inverse of −12. __12__

62 English Learner Support Guide • Algebra Readiness Practice 3

©Copyright SRA/McGraw-Hill. Permission is granted to reproduce this page for classroom use.

Practice 3, p.62

3 Reflect

Extended Response

- **What is a reciprocal?**
- **How is a reciprocal the same as an inverse?**
- **What is the difference between a multiplicative inverse and an additive inverse?**

Encourage student discussion of these questions and answers.

4 Assess

Informal Assessment

Have students complete the following activity to make sure they understand the vocabulary. As students use each word:

1. Check understanding.
2. Correct errors.
3. Recheck for understanding.

- Have students define *reciprocal* and *inverse* and explain how they differ.

For each word, use the following rubric to assign a score.

The student can repeat the word when prompted. (1 point)

The student knows the word but does not know its meaning. (2 points)

The student has a vague idea of the word's meaning. (3 points)

The student knows the word and can use the word in context. (4 points)

Final Assessment

Distribute a copy of the Final Assessment, p. 63, to each student. Use the following rubric to determine each student's level of English development.

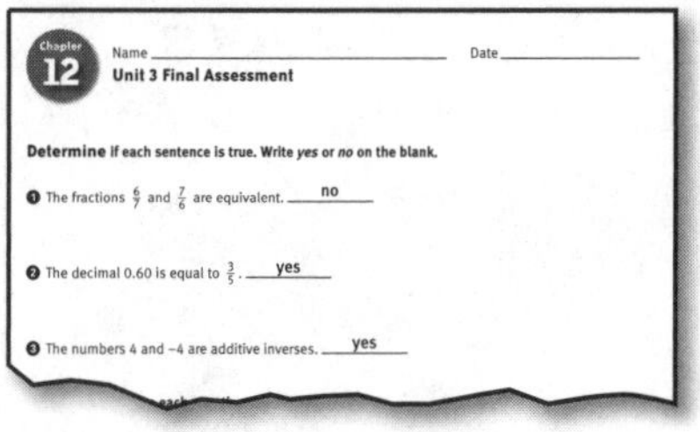

Chapter 12 Name ______ Date ______
Unit 3 Final Assessment

Determine if each sentence is true. Write *yes* or *no* on the blank.

1. The fractions $\frac{6}{7}$ and $\frac{7}{6}$ are equivalent. __no__
2. The decimal 0.60 is equal to $\frac{3}{5}$. __yes__
3. The numbers 4 and −4 are additive inverses. __yes__

Final Assessment, p. 63

- **Beginning English Learners:** 0–2 of Questions 1–6 correct
- **Intermediate English Learners:** 3–4 of Questions 1–6 correct
- **Advanced English Learners:** 5–6 of Questions 1–6 correct

  Use the Student Assessment Record, page 144, to record the assessment results.

Chapter 12

Name ______________________ Date ____________

Practice 1

Circle **each answer.**

1. Circle the numerator. $\frac{5}{7}$

2. Circle the sum. $5.5 + 4.2 = 9.7$

Determine **if each sentence is true. Write** ***yes*** **or** ***no*** **on the blank.**

3. $\frac{3}{4}$ **and** $\frac{6}{8}$ These fractions are equal. ____________

4. The number $\frac{19}{4}$ is a rational number. ____________

5. The reciprocal of $\frac{7}{8}$ is $-\frac{7}{8}$ ____________

Chapter 12

Name ______________________ Date ______________

Practice 2

Write your answers in complete sentences. Be ready to share your answers with the class.

1. $\frac{1}{4}$ **and** $\frac{5}{6}$ Are these numbers equal?

____

2. $\frac{14}{17}$ Is this a rational number?

____

3. $\frac{2}{7}$ **and** $\frac{7}{2}$ What are these numbers called?

____

4. $\frac{5}{8}$ What is an equivalent percent for this fraction?

____

5. **25** What is the additive inverse?

____

6. $\frac{15}{16}$ What number is the numerator?

____

Chapter 12

Name ______________________ Date ____________

Practice 3

Read each sentence below, and follow the directions carefully.

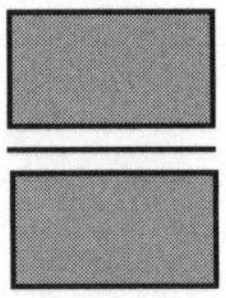

1. Write a 3 as the numerator of the fraction.

2. Write a 4 as the denominator of the fraction.

3. Write the fraction as a decimal. ____________

4. Write the decimal as a percent. ____________

5. Is $\frac{5}{6}$ equal to the fraction above? Write *yes* or *no*. ____________

6. Is $\frac{6}{8}$ is equal to the fraction above? Write *yes* or *no*. ____________

7. Write the reciprocal of the fraction. ____________

8. Write the additive inverse of -12. ____________

Chapter 12

Name ______________________ Date ______________

Unit 3 Final Assessment

Determine if each sentence is true. Write *yes* or *no* on the blank.

1. The fractions $\frac{6}{7}$ and $\frac{7}{6}$ are equivalent. ____________

2. The decimal 0.60 is equal to $\frac{3}{5}$. ____________

3. The numbers 4 and −4 are additive inverses. ____________

Write the answer to each question.

4. What is the reciprocal of $\frac{3}{4}$? ____________

5. **13 = 4 + 9** What are the addends? ____________

6. **44 ÷ 11 = 4** What is the quotient? ____________

Symbolic Notation/ Equations and Functions

Unit at a Glance

In this unit, students will learn the vocabulary associated with ***Number Worlds***, Algebra Readiness, Symbolic Notation/Equations and Functions. In this unit, students will evaluate expressions using parentheses, more than two terms, and different operations; evaluate symbols in expressions and equations; write and solve one- and two-step linear equations with one variable; evaluate and create solution sets for two-variable equations by determining a second number when a first number is given; simplify expressions by applying properties of rational numbers; and solve multistep problems involving rate, average speed, distance, and time or a direct variation. Before beginning the unit, assess students' general knowledge of math and vocabulary using the Individual Oral Assessment on page 65.

How Students Learn Vocabulary

Using visuals and manipulatives creates familiarity for English learners and has an immediate impact on learning language. For this unit, it will be helpful to have balance scales and Counters on hand so students can visualize the reality of the operations they will be conducting. Students will also benefit greatly from ample speaking practice. As much as possible, have students work with a partner or in groups of three to maximize opportunities for using new vocabulary.

Academic Vocabulary Taught in Unit 4

Chapter 13	Chapter 14	Chapter 15	Chapter 16
equation A mathematical statement showing that one quantity or expression is equal to another quantity or expression **evaluate** To establish the value or amount of an expression **expression** A group of mathematical symbols (numbers, operations signs, variables, grouping symbols) that represents a number **parentheses** A symbol separating one expression and/or operation from others	**constant** A value that remains the same, such as 3 in the expression $3 + x$ **function** A relationship that pairs every element of one set with an element of a second set; for example, a relationship that pairs any number with another number **line** A straight path that extends infinitely in opposite directions, thought of as having length, but no thickness **variable** A symbol that represents a quantity	**balanced equation** An equation such that both sides of the equal sign have the same quantity **solution set** The set of all values that satisfy an equation **table** An orderly arrangement of facts or information, usually in a list	**associative** Relating to a law stating that the sum or product of two or more quantities will be the same regardless of how they are grouped **commutative** Relating to a law stating that the sum or product of two or more quantities will be the same regardless of order **simplify** Applying operations and properties in order to make an expression or equation easier to evaluate or solve

Unit 4 Individual Oral Assessment

Directions: Read each question to the student, and record his or her oral responses. Some questions have teacher directions. Teacher directions are indicated in italics. Allow students to use pencil and paper to work their responses.

1. Is this an **expression**? *Show student a function table.* no

2. Is this an **expression**? *Write* $x - 7$ *on a piece of paper.* yes

3. Is this an **equation**? *Write* $x + 7 = 9$ *on a piece of paper.* yes

4. Is this a **function**? *Write* $x - 7 = y$ *on a piece of paper.* yes

5. Is 7 a **constant** or a **variable**? constant

6. Point to a **variable** in the **function**. Student should point to either the *x* or the *y*.

7. Is this a **line** or a **table**? *Show student a straight line.* a line

8. Is this a **line** or a **table**? *Show student a table.* table

9. Is this a **function** or an **expression**? *Write* $(x \times 4) \times 3 = y$ *on a piece of paper.* function

10. Are these **parentheses** or exponents? *Show student the same function, and point to the parentheses.* parentheses

11. In the **function**, if *x* equals 2, what does *y* equal? *Show student the same function.* 24

12. Is this the **associative** property or the **commutative** property? *Write* $(x \times 4) \times 3 = x \times (4 \times 3)$ *on a piece of paper.* associative property

13. Is this the **associative** property or the **commutative** property? *Write* $4 \times x \times 3 = \ \times 4 \times 3$ *on a piece of paper.* commutative property

- **Beginning English Learners:** 0–3 of Questions 1–10 correct
- **Intermediate English Learners:** 4–7 of Questions 1–10 correct
- **Advanced English Learners:** 8–10 of Questions 1–10 correct
- If the student is able to answer Questions 11–13, then he or she can understand the mathematics taught in this unit, but may still have difficulty with the academic vocabulary.

Use the Student Assessment Record, page 144, to record the assessment results.

Objective

Students can understand the meanings of the terms *expression*, *equation*, *evaluate*, and *parentheses*.

Materials

Program Materials

Expressions and Equations, p. 129

Additional Materials

Balance scale

Vocabulary

equation A mathematical statement showing that one quantity or expression is equal to another quantity or expression

evaluate To establish the value or amount of an expression

expression A group of mathematical symbols (numbers, operations signs, variables, grouping symbols) that represents a number

parentheses A symbol separating one expression and/or operation from others

1 Warm Up

Introduce each vocabulary word to students.
Say the word aloud.
Have students repeat the word.

Show students a balance scale. Say *balance scale,* and have students repeat the term. Demonstrate balance by putting identical objects on each side of the scale. Then show students what happens when you put objects of different weights on the scale.

Organize students into groups. Distribute a balance scale to each group. Allow students to experiment with the scales. Encourage students to find objects that are different but have equal weights. Tell students that although the items may be different, they are equivalent in weight. Say *equivalent,* and have students repeat the word. Write *equivalent* on the board.

2 Engage

Write 6, 3 + 3, $\frac{18}{3}$, and 2 × 3 on the board.

- **Which of these are equal?** all of them

Now change the expressions on the board as follows: 6, x + 3, $\frac{18}{x}$, and 2 × x.

- **Are these still equal?** Answers will vary.

Tell students that these are four different expressions for the same number. An expression is a group of mathematical symbols that represents a number. Say *expression,* and have students repeat the word. Write *expression* on the board.

Write 6 = x + 3 on the board. Point to the 6.

- **Is this an expression?** yes

Point to x + 3.

- **Is this an expression?** yes

Point to the equal sign.

- **Do the two sides equal each other?** yes

Tell students that when two equivalent expressions are on either side of an equal sign, it is called an equation. Say *equation,* and have students repeat the word. Write *equation* on the board.

Write 2 × 4 + 5 on the board.

- **Is this an expression?** yes
- **What is the answer?** Some students may answer 13, and others may answer 18.

Tell students that when they try to figure out the value of a number sentence or expression, they evaluate it. Say *evaluate,* and have students repeat the word. Write *evaluate* on the board.

Now draw parentheses around the first two numbers in the expression on the board: (2 × 4) + 5. Point to the parentheses, and say *parentheses.* Have students repeat the word. Tell students that when they see parentheses, they should do that operation first. Write *parentheses* on the board.

- **When we evaluate the expression, what do the parentheses tell us?** to do that operation first
- **What is the value of this expression?** 13

Distribute a copy of Expressions and Equations, p. 129, to each student. Organize students into pairs. Have partners complete the worksheet and review with another pair while you monitor.

Teacher's Note

English has many words that have multiple meanings. English learners need to know that context can help them understand word meaning. Encourage students to look for clarification if they are not sure what something means. The word *expression* has a number of meanings. Because the context in this lesson is math, *expression* refers to a group of mathematical symbols that represents a number, not a way of speaking that shows a feeling or a common word or group of words such as *look before you leap*.

Progress Monitoring

If . . .	Then . . .
If . . . students need additional practice with the vocabulary,	**Then . . .** have partners create and describe a list of equivalent expressions, such as 9, $6 + 3$, 3×3, and $10 - 1$.

3 Reflect

Extended Response

- **What does *express* mean? How does the term *express* relate to the word *expression*?**
- **How is a balance scale like an equal sign?**
- **Give an example of how equations are useful in the real world.**
- **Of what other words does *equation* remind you?**

Encourage student discussion of these questions and answers.

Progress Monitoring

If . . .	Then . . .
If . . . students seem slow to respond in the Extended Response activity,	**Then . . .** give them a little extra time to formulate their answers, or conduct the activity in pairs or groups to maximize speaking opportunities.

4 Assess

Informal Assessment

Have students complete the activity below to make sure they understand the vocabulary. As students use each word:

1. Check understanding.
2. Correct errors.
3. Recheck for understanding.

- Write $2x + (8 - 5) = 15$ on the board. Have students identify expressions and the equation.
- Have students evaluate the expression and describe their process, using the terms *expression, equation, evaluate,* and *parentheses.*

For each word, use the following rubric to assign a score.

The student can repeat the word when prompted. (1 point)

The student knows the word but does not know its meaning. (2 points)

The student has a vague idea of the word's meaning. (3 points)

The student knows the word and can use the word in context. (4 points)

Chapter 14

Unit 4 • Symbolic Notation/Equations and Functions

Objective

Students can understand the meanings of the terms *variable, constant, function,* and *line.*

Materials

Program Materials

Vocabulary Cards 13 (function) and 49 (variable)

Vocabulary

constant A value that remains the same, such as 3 in the expression 3 + *x*

function A relationship that pairs every element of one set with an element of a second set; for example, a relationship that pairs any number with another number

line A straight path that extends infinitely in opposite directions, thought of as having length, but no thickness

variable A symbol that represents a quantity

1 Warm Up

Introduce each vocabulary word to students.
Say the word aloud.
Have students repeat the word.

After students have listened to the words, show them ***Vocabulary Cards* 13** and **49**.

Write 4 + 5 on the board.

- **Is this an expression?** yes
- **Evaluate it.** It equals nine.

Write 4 + 5 = 9 on the board. Underline the entire equation.

- **Is this an expression?** no
- **What is it called?** an equation

Repeat with other expressions and equations until students are comfortable with the difference between *expressions* and *equations*.

2 Engage

Write 9, 3 + 6, $\frac{27}{3}$, and 3 × 3 on the board.

- **Which of these are equivalent?** all of them

Now change the expressions on the board as follows: 9, x + 6, $\frac{27}{x}$, x × 3.

- **Are these still equivalent?** Answers will vary.

Tell students that these are four different expressions for the same number. An expression is a group of mathematical symbols that represents a number. Say *expression,* and have students repeat the word. Write *expression* on the board.

- **If all these expressions are equivalent, what dose x equal?** 3

Point to the expression x + 6.

- **Is this an expression?** yes
- **If x = 1, what does x + 6 equal?** 7

Repeat for x = 2, 3, 4, and 5.

Tell students that the value of x can change. Because of this, it is called a variable. Say *variable,* and have students repeat the word. Write *variable* on the board.

Return to the expression x + 6.

- **Is the number 6 a variable?** no
- **How do you know?** because its value does not change

Tell students that a number whose value never changes is called a constant. Say *constant,* and have students repeat the word. Write *constant* on the board.

Write x + 6 = y on the board. Tell students that a function is an equation in which a value is paired with another value. Say *function,* and have students repeat the word. Write *function* on the board.

Have partners find the value for y if x equals 1, 2, 3, 4, and 5. Write students' findings in a table on the board. Plot the resulting points on a coordinate grid on the board or on an overhead transparency. Draw a straight line connecting the points.

- **What is this?** a line

Say *line,* and have students repeat the word. Write *line* on the board.

Teacher's Note

English learners may already understand the mathematical concepts being taught but lack the English vocabulary to express them. Use this to your advantage when introducing words by allowing students to describe this process in their primary language before they describe the process in English.

Progress Monitoring

If . . . students confuse constants and variables,	**Then . . .** remind them that *variable* means "changing," and *constant* means "unchanging."

3 Reflect

Extended Response

- **What does *vary* mean? What does *variety* mean?**
- **Explain what a variable is.**
- **Can a fraction be a constant? Why or why not?**
- **How do we use functions every day?**

Encourage student discussion of these questions and answers.

Progress Monitoring

If . . . students are having trouble using the math vocabulary they have learned,	**Then . . .** work with them individually or in small groups.

4 Assess

Informal Assessment

Have students complete the activity below to make sure they understand the vocabulary. As students use each word:

1. Check understanding.
2. Correct errors.
3. Recheck for understanding.

- Write the expression $x - 7$ on the board. Have students identify the variable and the constant.
- Have students determine the value of x to make the expression equivalent to 10.
- Have students define *function* in their own words. Write the equation $x + 5 = y$. Have students determine the value for y if x equals 1, 2, 3, 4, and 5.

For each word, use the following rubric to assign a score.

The student can repeat the word when prompted. (1 point)

The student knows the word but does not know its meaning. (2 points)

The student has a vague idea of the word's meaning. (3 points)

The student knows the word and can use the word in context. (4 points)

Objective

Students can understand the meanings of the terms *table, solution set,* and *balanced equation.*

Materials

Program Materials

Function Tables, p. 130

Additional Materials

Balance scales

Vocabulary

balanced equation An equation such that both sides of the equal sign have the same quantity

solution set The set of all values that satisfy an equation

table An orderly arrangement of facts or information, usually in a list

1 Warm Up

Introduce each vocabulary word to students.
Say the word aloud.
Have students repeat the word.

As a brief activity, have students brainstorm a list of fruits and possible prices for each. Then have them tell you how much five of each fruit would cost. Discuss how much ten of each fruit would cost.

Use one of the examples from the brainstorming activity, and write the function on the board. For example, each apple costs five cents. Write a function for the cost of apples: $x \times 5¢ = y¢$. Tell students that this is a function for the cost of apples. Have students identify the variables and constants in the function.

2 Engage

Help students discover that we can change the function by changing one of the numbers.

- **What represents the cost per apple?** 5¢
- **What represents the number of apples?** *x*
- **How can I show how much five apples will cost?** Change the *x* to 5.
- **How much do five apples cost?** 25¢
- **How can I show how much seven apples will cost?** Change the *x* to 7.
- **How much do seven apples cost?** 35¢
- **How can I show how much ten apples will cost?** Change the *x* to 10.
- **How much do ten apples cost?** 50¢

Repeat the question with other numbers until students discover that changing the number of apples (x) changes the total cost of the apples (y).

Draw a function table on the board, and complete the table as students supply the information. Say *table,* and have students repeat the word. Write *table* on the board.

After you have finished, tell students that the information is called a solution set because it gives a group of values for the function. Say *solution set,* and have students repeat the term. Write *solution set* on the board.

Also have students notice that each time the value of one variable changes, the value of the other variable also changes. This is called a balanced equation. Say *balanced equation,* and have students repeat the term. Write *balanced equation* on the board.

Demonstrate the idea of balance using a balance scale. Put identical objects on each side of the scale to show balance. Then show students what happens when objects of different weights are put on the scale.

Organize students into pairs. Distribute a balance scale to each pair of students. Allow partners to experiment with the scales. Encourage students to find objects that are different but have equal weights.

Distribute a copy of Function Tables, p. 130, to each student. Have students work with their partner to complete the worksheet. Review answers as a class. Encourage students to discuss their differences.

Teacher's Note

Students may struggle to think of examples and answers to the following Extended Response questions. Be prepared with a few examples of your own to get students started.

Progress Monitoring

If . . .	Then . . .
If . . . students need extra practice with the vocabulary and the mathematical concepts,	**Then . . .** have students work with a partner to create functions and tables for the cost of other fruits on their lists.

3 Reflect

Extended Response

- **How is a table useful?**
- **How is using a balance scale like writing an equation?**
- **When a variable in an equation changes, what happens to the value of the other variable?**
- **How big is a solution set?**

Encourage student discussion of these questions and answers.

Progress Monitoring

If . . .	Then . . .
If . . . students seem to understand the mathematical idea but are having trouble with appropriate use of vocabulary,	**Then . . .** review the vocabulary with students individually.

4 Assess

Informal Assessment

Have students complete the activity below to make sure they understand the vocabulary. As students use each word:

1. Check understanding.
2. Correct errors.
3. Recheck for understanding.

- Have students select a value for the input and compute the output using the function rule $x \times 3 = y$.
- Have students create a solution set for the equation.
- Have students describe the process using the terms *solution set* and *balanced equation.*

For each word, use the following rubric to assign a score.

The student can repeat the word when prompted. (1 point)

The student knows the word but does not know its meaning. (2 points)

The student has a vague idea of the word's meaning. (3 points)

The student knows the word and can use the word in context. (4 points)

Chapter 16

Unit 4 • Symbolic Notation/Equations and Functions

Objective

Students can understand the meanings of the terms *simplify*, *associative*, and *commutative*.

Materials

Program Materials

Two-Color Counters

Vocabulary

associative Relating to a law stating that the sum or product of two or more quantities will be the same regardless of how they are grouped

commutative Relating to a law stating that the sum or product of two or more quantities will be the same regardless of order

simplify Applying operations and properties in order to make an expression or equation easier to evaluate or solve

1 Warm Up

Introduce each vocabulary word to students.
Say the word aloud.
Have students repeat the word.

Write $2 \times 6 = 12$ on the board. Point to the 12.

- **What is this called? Is it a product or a factor?** product

Point to the 6.

- **What is this called? Is it a product or a factor?** factor

Distribute 12 Counters to each student. Have students arrange Counters in two groups of six. Then have them use their Counters to discover other factors of 12.

2 Engage

Write $6 \times 4 = ?$ on the board. Distribute an additional 12 Counters to each student. Have students put their Counters in six groups of four.

- **What is the product?** The product is 24.
- **What are the factors?** The factors are 4 and 6.

Write $4 \times 6 = 24$ on the board.

Have students put their Counters in four groups of six.

- **What is the product?** The product is 24.
- **What are the factors?** The factors are 6 and 4.

Write $6 \times 4 = 24$ on the board.

- **Do 6×4 and 4×6 have the same answer?** yes

Tell students that the order of factors does not affect the product. This property is called the commutative property of multiplication. Say *commutative property of multiplication*, and have students repeat the term. Write *commutative property of multiplication* on the board.

Write $(2 \times 2) \times 6 = ?$ on the board. Have students arrange Counters in two groups of two.

- **How many Counters do you have?** four

Write $4 \times 6 = 24$ on the board below $(2 \times 2) \times 6 = ?$ Have students arrange Counters in four groups of six.

- **How many Counters do you have now?** twenty-four

Write $2 \times (2 \times 6) = ?$ on the board next to $(2 \times 2) \times 6 = ?$ Have students arrange Counters in two groups of six.

- **How many Counters do you have?** twelve

Write $2 \times 12 = 24$ on the board below $2 \times (2 \times 6) = ?$ Have students arrange Counters in two groups of twelve.

- **How many Counters do you have now?** twenty-four
- **Is the answer the same when the factors are grouped differently?** yes

Tell students that when adding or multiplying three or more numbers, the order in which they are grouped does not matter. This property is called the associative property of multiplication. Say *associative property of multiplication*, and have students repeat the term. Write *associative property of multiplication* on the board.

- **Why do we use these properties?** Answers will vary.

Tell students that these properties are useful because they make solving the problem easier. This is called simplifying. Say *simplify*, and have students repeat the word. Write *simplify* on the board.

Teacher's Note

The vocabulary in this lesson may be difficult for English learners to pronounce. Give students ample opportunities for practice, on an individual and group basis.

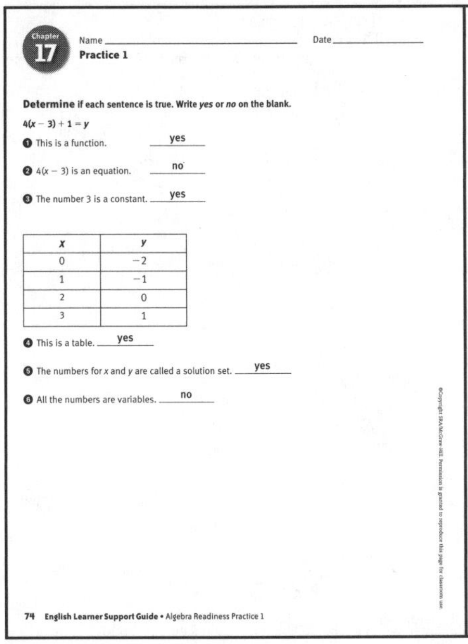

Chapter 17 Name ______ Date ______
Practice 1

Determine if each sentence is true. Write *yes* or *no* on the blank.

$4(x - 3) + 1 = y$

1. This is a function. yes
2. $4(x - 3)$ is an equation. no
3. The number 3 is a constant. yes

x	y
0	−2
1	−1
2	0
3	1

4. This is a table. yes
5. The numbers for x and y are called a solution set. yes
6. All the numbers are variables. no

74 **English Learner Support Guide** • Algebra Readiness Practice 1

Practice 1, p. 74

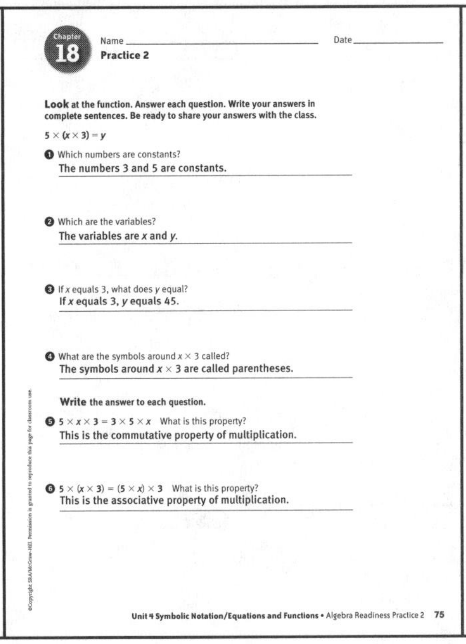

Chapter 18 Name ______ Date ______
Practice 2

Look at the function. Answer each question. Write your answers in complete sentences. Be ready to share your answers with the class.

$5 \times (x \times 3) = y$

1. Which numbers are constants?
   The numbers 3 and 5 are constants.
2. Which are the variables?
   The variables are x and y.
3. If x equals 3, what does y equal?
   If x equals 3, y equals 45.
4. What are the symbols around $x \times 3$ called?
   The symbols around $x \times 3$ are called parentheses.

Write the answer to each question.

5. $5 \times x \times 3 = 3 \times 5 \times x$ What is this property?
   This is the commutative property of multiplication.
6. $5 \times (x \times 3) = (5 \times x) \times 3$ What is this property?
   This is the associative property of multiplication.

Unit 4 Symbolic Notation/Equations and Functions • Algebra Readiness Practice 2 75

Practice 2, p. 75

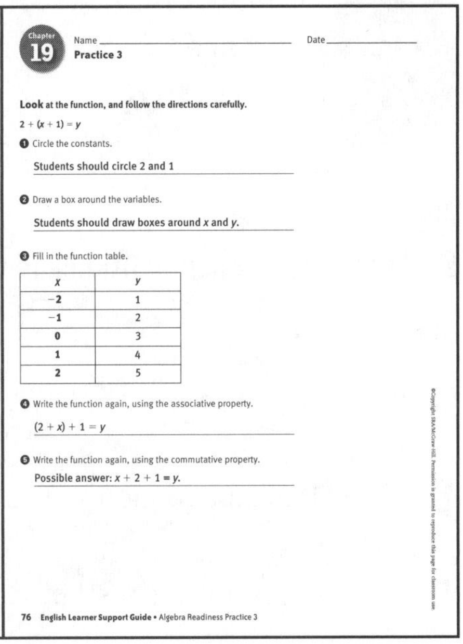

Chapter 19 Name ______ Date ______
Practice 3

Look at the function, and follow the directions carefully.

$2 + (x + 1) = y$

1. Circle the constants.
   Students should circle 2 and 1
2. Draw a box around the variables.
   Students should draw boxes around x and y.
3. Fill in the function table.

x	y
−2	1
−1	2
0	3
1	4
2	5

4. Write the function again, using the associative property.
   $(2 + x) + 1 = y$
5. Write the function again, using the commutative property.
   Possible answer: $x + 2 + 1 = y$.

76 **English Learner Support Guide** • Algebra Readiness Practice 3

Practice 3, p. 76

Using Student Worksheets

After students complete the activity, help them to complete the appropriate Practice for their levels of English development.

Level 1, Practice 1, p. 74

Level 2, Practice 2, p. 75

Level 3, Practice 3, p. 46

3 Reflect

Extended Response

- **Describe the associative property of multiplication.**
- **Why are the commutative and associative properties useful?**
- **Why do we simplify problems?**

Encourage student discussion of these questions and answers.

4 Assess

Informal Assessment

Have students complete the following activity to make sure they understand the vocabulary. As students use each word:

1. Check understanding.
2. Correct errors.
3. Recheck for understanding.

- Write $9 \times 3 = 3 \times 9$ on the board. Have students identify the appropriate property.
- Write $(9 \times 3) \times 2 = 9 \times (3 \times 2)$ on the board. Have students identify the appropriate property.

For each word, use the following rubric to assign a score.

The student can repeat the word when prompted. (1 point)

The student knows the word but does not know its meaning. (2 points)

The student has a vague idea of the word's meaning. (3 points)

The student knows the word and can use the word in context. (4 points)

Final Assessment

Distribute a copy of the Final Assessment, p. 77, to each student. Use the following rubric to determine each student's level of English development.

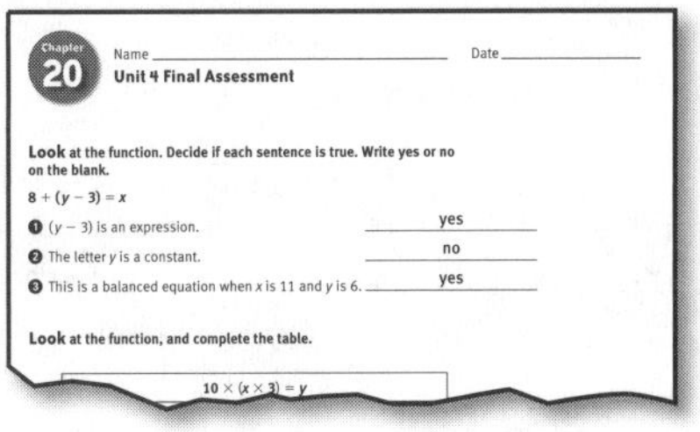

Chapter 20 Name ______ Date ______
Unit 4 Final Assessment

Look at the function. Decide if each sentence is true. Write yes or no on the blank.

$8 + (y - 3) = x$

1. $(y - 3)$ is an expression. yes
2. The letter y is a constant. no
3. This is a balanced equation when x is 11 and y is 6. yes

Look at the function, and complete the table.

$10 \times (x \times 3) = y$

Final Assessment, p. 77

- **Beginning English Learners:** 0–2 of Questions 1–6 correct
- **Intermediate English Learners:** 3–4 of Questions 1–6 correct
- **Advanced English Learners:** 5–6 of Questions 1–6 correct

Use the Student Assessment Record, page 144, to record the assessment results.

Chapter 17

Name ______________________ Date ____________

Practice 1

Determine if each sentence is true. Write *yes* or *no* on the blank.

$4(x - 3) + 1 = y$

1. This is a function. ____________

2. $4(x - 3)$ is an equation. ____________

3. The number 3 is a constant. ____________

x	y
0	−2
1	−1
2	0
3	1

4. This is a table. ____________

5. The numbers for x and y are called a solution set. ____________

6. All the numbers are variables. ____________

Chapter 18

Name ____________________ Date ____________

Practice 2

Look at the function. Answer each question. Write your answers in complete sentences. Be ready to share your answers with the class.

$5 \times (x \times 3) = y$

1. Which numbers are constants?

____

2. Which are the variables?

____

3. If x equals 3, what does y equal?

____

4. What are the symbols around $x \times 3$ called?

____

Write the answer to each question.

5. $5 \times x \times 3 = 3 \times 5 \times x$ What is this property?

____

6. $5 \times (x \times 3) = (5 \times x) \times 3$ What is this property?

____

Name ______________________ Date ____________

Practice 3

Look at the function, and follow the directions carefully.

$2 + (x + 1) = y$

1. Circle the constants.

____

2. Draw a box around the variables.

____

3. Fill in the function table.

x	*y*
−2	
−1	
0	
1	
2	

4. Write the function again, using the associative property.

____

5. Write the function again, using the commutative property.

____

Name ______________________ Date ____________

Unit 4 Final Assessment

Look at the function. Decide if each sentence is true. Write yes or no on the blank.

$8 + (y - 3) = x$

1. $(y - 3)$ is an expression. ____________
2. The letter y is a constant. ____________
3. This is a balanced equation when x is 11 and y is 6. ____________

Look at the function, and complete the table.

	$10 \times (x \times 3) = y$	
	x	y
4	3	
5	4	
6	5	

The Coordinate Plane and Graphing

Unit at a Glance

In this unit, students will learn the vocabulary associated with ***Number Worlds***, Algebra Readiness, The Coordinate Plane and Graphing. In this unit, students will understand the coordinate plane, explore the Pythagorean theorem, understand functions and know how to graph them on a coordinate plane, and understand rates and dimensional analysis. Before beginning the unit, assess students' general knowledge of math and vocabulary using the Individual Oral Assessment on page 79.

How Students Learn Vocabulary

Using visuals and manipulatives creates familiarity for English learners and has an immediate impact on learning language. For this unit, it will be helpful to have clock faces, attribute blocks, graph paper, and scissors on hand so students can visualize the reality of the operations they will be conducting. Having students create their own examples of new vocabulary is another useful way to connect students to the reality of what they are learning.

Academic Vocabulary Taught in Unit 5

Chapter 17	Chapter 18	Chapter 19	Chapter 20
coordinate grid A grid used to locate points according to their distances from two perpendicular number lines **ordered pair** Two numbers written so that one is considered before the other; coordinates of points are written as ordered pairs, with the *x*-coordinate written first, and then the *y*-coordinate **plot the points** Locate where the points intersect and mark them on a graph ***x*-axis** The horizontal axis of a coordinate graph ***y*-axis** The vertical axis of a coordinate graph	**hypotenuse** The side of a right triangle opposite the right angle **line segment** A part of a line with two endpoints **Pythagorean theorem** Named for the Greek mathematician Pythagoras; for any right triangle, the square of the length of the hypotenuse is equal to the sum of the squares of the lengths of the other two sides. It is written as $a^2 + b^2 = c^2$, where c is the length of the hypotenuse, and a and b are the lengths of the other sides **right angle** An angle measuring 90 degrees	**horizontal** Of or relating to the horizon **slope** A ratio that indicates the steepness of a line; the tangent of the angle made by a straight line with the *x*-axis **vertical** Perpendicular to the horizon	**dimensional analysis** A manner of multiplying conversion factors to generate an answer of the appropriate unit **rate** A ratio comparing two quantities with unlike units **ratio** The comparison of two numbers by division **unit rate** A rate with a denominator of one

Unit 5 Individual Oral Assessment

Directions: Read each question to the student, and record his or her oral responses. Some questions have teacher directions. Teacher directions are indicated in italics. Allow students to use pencil and paper to work their responses.

1. Does this have a **right angle**? *Show student a triangle attribute block that has no right angle.* **no**
2. Is this a **rate**? *Write* 20 miles/hour *on a piece of paper.* **yes**
3. Is this a **coordinate grid**? *Show student a coordinate grid with a line that has slope.* **yes**
4. Point to the ***x*-axis**. **Student should point to the *x*-axis.**
5. Point to the ***y*-axis**. **Student should point to the *y*-axis.**
6. Does this line have **slope**? **yes**
7. Describe a **vertical** line. **A line that goes up and down; a line that is perpendicular to the horizon.**
8. Is this a **unit rate** or a **ratio**? *Write* 7:8 *on a piece of paper.* **ratio**
9. What is a **unit rate**? **a rate with a denominator of one**
10. What is an **ordered pair**? **Two numbers written so that one is considered before the other; for example, coordinates of points such as (2, 12).**
11. Point to the **right angle**. *Show student a right triangle with two sides labeled* 3 *and* 4. **Student should point to the right angle.**
12. Point to the **hypotenuse**. **Student should point to the hypotenuse.**
13. If a car goes 100 miles in two hours, what is its **rate**? **50 miles per hour**

- **Beginning English Learners:** 0–3 of Questions 1–10 correct
- **Intermediate English Learners:** 4–7 of Questions 1–10 correct
- **Advanced English Learners:** 8–10 of Questions 1–10 correct
- If the student is able to answer Questions 11–13, then he or she can understand the mathematics taught in this unit, but may still have difficulty with the academic vocabulary.

Use the Student Assessment Record, page 144, to record the assessment results.

Objective

Students can understand the meanings of the terms *ordered pair, coordinate grid, x-axis, y-axis,* and *plot the points.*

Materials

Program Materials

- Vocabulary Card 23 (ordered pair)
- Graphing Variables, p. 131

Vocabulary

coordinate grid A grid used to locate points according to their distances from two perpendicular number lines

ordered pair Two numbers written so that one is considered before the other; coordinates of points are written as ordered pairs, with the *x*-coordinate written first, and then the *y*-coordinate

plot the points Locate where the points intersect and mark them on a graph

***x*-axis** The horizontal axis of a coordinate graph

***y*-axis** The vertical axis of a coordinate graph

1 Warm Up

Introduce each vocabulary word to students.
Say the word aloud.
Have students repeat the word.

After students have listened to the words, show them ***Vocabulary Card 23,*** and have them say the word again.

To review the lesson vocabulary from the last unit, remind students of the functions they created to determine the total cost of fruit. Have them create a new function for the cost of oranges, assuming that each orange costs seven cents. They should come up with x *(number of oranges)* × 7¢ = y¢.

- **What is this called?** function
- **What are the variables in this function?** x and y
- **What does x mean?** number of oranges
- **What does y mean?** total cost of oranges
- **Which value in the function never changes?** 7¢
- **What is that called?** a constant

2 Engage

Continue with the previous example.

- **What happens if I change x to 5?** The function changes to 5 *oranges* × 7¢ = 35¢.

Distribute a copy of Graphing Variables, p. 131, to each student. Organize students into pairs. Have partners substitute the numbers 1, 2, 3, 4, 6, 7, and 8 for x in the orange function and complete the two-column table for the function on the worksheet. Review the worksheet as a group.

- **If x equals 1, what does y equal?** 7¢

Write *(1, 7)* on the board. Tell students that this is called an ordered pair. The first value is the x-value, and the second value is always the y-value. Say *ordered pair,* and have students repeat the term. Write *ordered pair* on the board.

Point out the coordinate grid on the worksheet. Tell students that ordered pairs are marked on a grid like this, called a coordinate grid. Say *coordinate grid,* and have students repeat the term. Write *coordinate grid* on the board.

Tell students that each number line on a coordinate grid is called an axis. Point to the horizontal axis, and tell students that this axis is called the *x-axis.* Say *x-axis,* and have students repeat the term. Write *x-axis* on the board. Label the *x-axis* on the grid on the board. Finally, tell students that the x-value in an ordered pair is marked along the x-axis. Repeat for the y-axis.

Demonstrate how to plot the points, or mark the ordered pairs, on the coordinate grid. Say *plot the points,* and have students repeat the term. Write *plot the points* on the board.

Have partners complete the worksheet by graphing the ordered pairs. Have each pair of students review their work with another pair as you monitor.

Teacher's Note

Allow students to work with a partner as often as possible. This maximizes opportunities for practicing English in a meaningful situation.

Progress Monitoring

If . . .	Then . . .
If . . . students are struggling with the new vocabulary,	**Then . . .** partner them with higher-performing students to practice using the vocabulary as they work the activities.

3 Reflect

Extended Response

- **What does the graph of the orange function show?**
- **How are graphs of functions useful?**
- **Why is the x variable always listed first in an ordered pair?**
- **What does *constant* mean?**

Encourage student discussion of these questions and answers.

Progress Monitoring

If . . .	Then . . .
If . . . students do not understand the vocabulary presented in this lesson,	**Then . . .** work with them individually to review.

4 Assess

Informal Assessment

Have students complete the activity below to make sure they understand the vocabulary. As students use each word:

1. Check understanding.
2. Correct errors.
3. Recheck for understanding.

- Have students describe and demonstrate how to use a function rule to determine ordered pairs.
- Have students describe and demonstrate how to graph ordered pairs on a coordinate grid.

For each word, use the following rubric to assign a score.

The student can repeat the word when prompted. (1 point)

The student knows the word but does not know its meaning. (2 points)

The student has a vague idea of the word's meaning. (3 points)

The student knows the word and can use the word in context. (4 points)

Objective

Students can understand the meanings of the terms *right angle, line segment, hypotenuse,* and *Pythagorean theorem.*

Materials

Program Materials

- Vocabulary Cards 14 (hypotenuse), 17 (line segment), 31 (Pythagorean theorem), and 39 (right angle)

Additional Materials

- Clock face with movable hands 
- Attribute blocks 
- Scissors

Vocabulary

hypotenuse The side of a right triangle opposite the right angle
line segment A part of a line with two endpoints
Pythagorean theorem Named for the Greek mathematician Pythagoras; for any right triangle, the square of the length of the hypotenuse is equal to the sum of the squares of the lengths of the other two sides. It is written as $a^2 + b^2 = c^2$, where c is the length of the hypotenuse, and a and b are the lengths of the other sides
right angle An angle measuring 90 degrees

1 Warm Up

Introduce each vocabulary word to students.
Say the word aloud.
Have students repeat the word.

Show students a clock face. Move clock hands to show 3:00. Put a small attribute block square at the intersection of the hands. Tell students that this is a right angle. Say *right angle*, and have students repeat the word. Write *right angle* on the board.

Move hands to 1:00.

- **Is this a right angle?** no

Move hands to 9:00.

- **Is this a right angle?** yes

Point to one of the clock hands.

- **Is this a line?** yes
- **Does it have an endpoint?** yes

Tell students that a line with two endpoints is called a line segment. Say *line segment*, and have students repeat the term. Write *line segment* on the board.

Now that students have had some experience with the words, show students ***Vocabulary Cards* 14, 17, 31,** and **39,** and say the words.

2 Engage

Organize students into pairs. Distribute several attribute blocks to each pair of students. Challenge them to locate as many blocks with right angles as they can.

Fold a sheet of paper in half from corner to diagonal corner. Have students watch as you carefully cut a piece of paper along the diagonal line. Hold up the resulting triangle.

- **What is this?** triangle
- **What do you notice about the triangle?** It has a right angle.

Tell students that they are correct, and that this triangle can be called a right triangle. Draw a right triangle on the board. Point out the line segments as you draw them.

Have students create their own right triangles using paper and scissors. Tell them to point to the right angle.

After monitoring to check students have correctly located the right angle, tell them to point to the side of the triangle that is opposite, or across from, the right angle. Tell them that this is called the hypotenuse. Say *hypotenuse*, and have students repeat the word. Label the hypotenuse on the board.

Introduce the Pythagorean theorem by labeling the length of the hypotenuse at 5 inches and the corresponding sides of the right triangle at 3 inches and 4 inches. Show students that the sum of the squares of the sides equals the square of the hypotenuse, or $3^2 + 4^2 = 5^2$. Tell them this is an example of the Pythagorean theorem. Say *Pythagorean theorem*, and have students repeat the term. Write *Pythagorean theorem* on the board.

Teacher's Note

Concept checking is an important part of teaching to English learners. When introducing vocabulary, ask questions to determine whether students understand the meanings of words and ideas. Ask concept-check questions to individual students and occasionally to the whole group.

Progress Monitoring

If . . .	Then . . .
If . . . students are confused about which side of a triangle is the hypotenuse,	**Then . . .** tell them that the hypotenuse is the side that does not form the right angle.

3 Reflect

Extended Response

- **Where do you see right angles in the classroom?**
- **Look outside. Where do you see right angles?**
- **What is a hypotenuse?**
- **If the sides of a right triangle are eight centimeters and six centimeters, how long is the hypotenuse?**

Encourage student discussion of these questions and answers.

Progress Monitoring

If . . .	Then . . .
If . . . you realize that a student has misunderstood a new vocabulary word,	**Then . . .** help the student with additional one-on-one practice. Using the word in free discussion is productive only when the student understands its meaning.

4 Assess

Informal Assessment

Have students complete the activity below to make sure they understand the vocabulary. As students use each word:

1. Check understanding.
2. Correct errors.
3. Recheck for understanding.

- Draw a right triangle on the board. Have students identify the right angle and the hypotenuse.
- Have students describe the Pythagorean theorem.

For each word, use the following rubric to assign a score.

The student can repeat the word when prompted. (1 point)

The student knows the word but does not know its meaning. (2 points)

The student has a vague idea of the word's meaning. (3 points)

The student knows the word and can use the word in context. (4 points)

Objective

Students can understand the meanings of the terms *slope*, *vertical*, and *horizontal*.

Materials

Program Materials

- Vocabulary Card 43 (slope)
- Vertical, Horizontal, or Slope? p. 132

Additional Materials

Graph paper

Vocabulary

horizontal Of or relating to the horizon
slope A ratio that indicates the steepness of a line; the tangent of the angle made by a straight line with the *x*-axis
vertical Perpendicular to the horizon

1 Warm Up

Introduce each vocabulary word to students.
Say the word aloud.
Have students repeat the word.

After students have listened to the vocabulary, show them ***Vocabulary Card 43***, and have them say the word again.

Review vocabulary from previous units and lessons. Write the following function on the board: $2x - 2 = y$.

Circle the entire function.

- **What is this called?** function

Circle the x.

- **What is this called?** variable

Circle the y.

- **What is this called?** variable

Point to the 2.

- **What is this called?** constant

Show students a coordinate grid on an overhead transparency.

- **What is this called?** coordinate grid

Point to the x-axis.

- **What is this called?** x-axis

Repeat for the y-axis.

2 Engage

Return to the function $2x - 2 = y$.

- **If we substitute the value of 1 for x, what is the value of y?** 0
- **So, if $x = 1$ and $y = 0$, what is the ordered pair?** (1, 0)

Repeat for x-values of 2, 3, 4, and 5. Plot the points on the coordinate grid. Have students plot the same points on their own graph paper.

Point out how plotted points can be connected with a straight line.

- **What is this called?** a line

Point to the slope of the line you created on the graph. Tell students that the steepness of the line is its slope. Say *slope*, and have students repeat the word. Write *slope* on the board.

Write the equation $x = 3$ on the board.

- **If $y = 0$, what does x equal?** 3

Repeat for y-values of 1, 2, 3, and 4, and create ordered pairs for each. Plot the points on the coordinate grid. Have students plot the same points and connect the points on their own graph paper.

- **What do you notice about the line?** It goes straight up and down; it is perpendicular to the x-axis.

Tell students that a line that goes straight up and down, or is perpendicular to the x-axis, is vertical. Say *vertical*, and have students repeat the word. Write *vertical* on the board.

Repeat for *horizontal*, using an equation such as $y = 2$.

Organize students into groups of three. Distribute a copy of Vertical, Horizontal, or Slope? p. 132, to each student. Have students work in groups to complete the worksheet. Review the worksheet as a class.

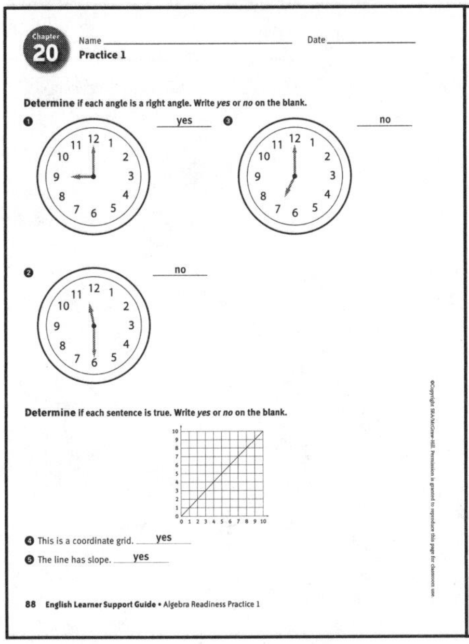

Chapter 20 Name Date
Practice 1

Determine if each angle is a right angle. Write *yes* or *no* on the blank.

1 yes 3 no

2 no

Determine if each sentence is true. Write *yes* or *no* on the blank.

4 This is a coordinate grid. yes

5 The line has slope. yes

88 English Learner Support Guide • Algebra Readiness Practice 1

Practice 1, p. 88

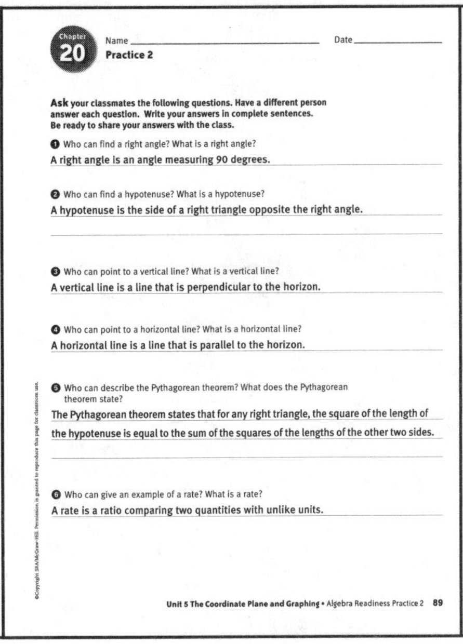

Chapter 20 Name Date
Practice 2

Ask your classmates the following questions. Have a different person answer each question. Write your answers in complete sentences. Be ready to share your answers with the class.

1 Who can find a right angle? What is a right angle?
A right angle is an angle measuring 90 degrees.

2 Who can find a hypotenuse? What is a hypotenuse?
A hypotenuse is the side of a right triangle opposite the right angle.

3 Who can point to a vertical line? What is a vertical line?
A vertical line is a line that is perpendicular to the horizon.

4 Who can point to a horizontal line? What is a horizontal line?
A horizontal line is a line that is parallel to the horizon.

5 Who can describe the Pythagorean theorem? What does the Pythagorean theorem state?
The Pythagorean theorem states that for any right triangle, the square of the length of the hypotenuse is equal to the sum of the squares of the lengths of the other two sides.

6 Who can give an example of a rate? What is a rate?
A rate is a ratio comparing two quantities with unlike units.

Unit 5 The Coordinate Plane and Graphing • Algebra Readiness Practice 2 89

Practice 2, p. 89

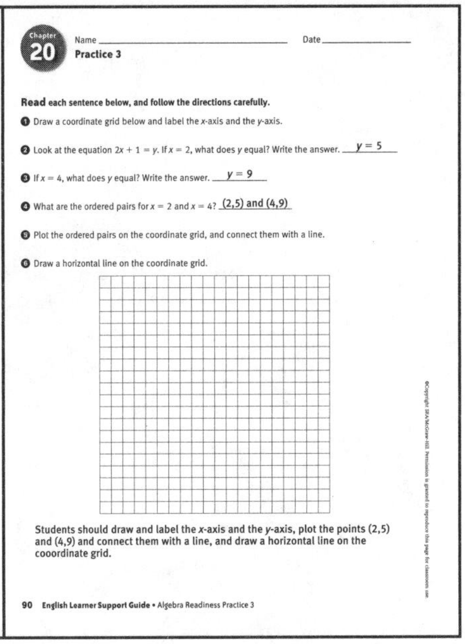

Chapter 20 Name Date
Practice 3

Read each sentence below, and follow the directions carefully.

1 Draw a coordinate grid below and label the *x*-axis and the *y*-axis.

2 Look at the equation $2x + 1 = y$. If $x = 2$, what does *y* equal? Write the answer. $y = 5$

3 If $x = 4$, what does *y* equal? Write the answer. $y = 9$

4 What are the ordered pairs for $x = 2$ and $x = 4$? (2,5) and (4,9)

5 Plot the ordered pairs on the coordinate grid, and connect them with a line.

6 Draw a horizontal line on the coordinate grid.

Students should draw and label the *x*-axis and the *y*-axis, plot the points (2,5) and (4,9) and connect them with a line, and draw a horizontal line on the cooordinate grid.

90 English Learner Support Guide • Algebra Readiness Practice 3

Practice 3, p. 90

Using Student Worksheets

After students complete the activity, help them complete the appropriate Practice for their levels of English development.

Level 1, Practice 1, p. 88

Level 2, Practice 2, p. 89

Level 3, Practice 3, p. 90

3 Reflect

Extended Response

- **How can we use a ratio to show how many girls are in the class?**
- **Suppose there are 20 students in the class, and 9 students are girls. What does the ratio 9:11 mean?**
- **What does the ratio $\frac{9}{20}$ mean?**
- **If kiwis are 6 for $3, what is the unit rate?**

Encourage student discussion of these questions and answers.

4 Assess

Informal Assessment

Have students complete the following activity to make sure they understand the vocabulary. As students use each word:

1. Check understanding.
2. Correct errors.
3. Recheck for understanding.

Have students define *ratio, rate,* and *unit rate* in their own words and give examples of each.

For each word, use the following rubric to assign a score.

The student can repeat the word when prompted. (1 point)

The student knows the word but does not know its meaning. (2 points)

The student has a vague idea of the word's meaning. (3 points)

The student knows the word and can use the word in context. (4 points)

Final Assessment

Distribute a copy of the Final Assessment, p. 91, to each student. Use the following rubric to determine each student's level of English development.

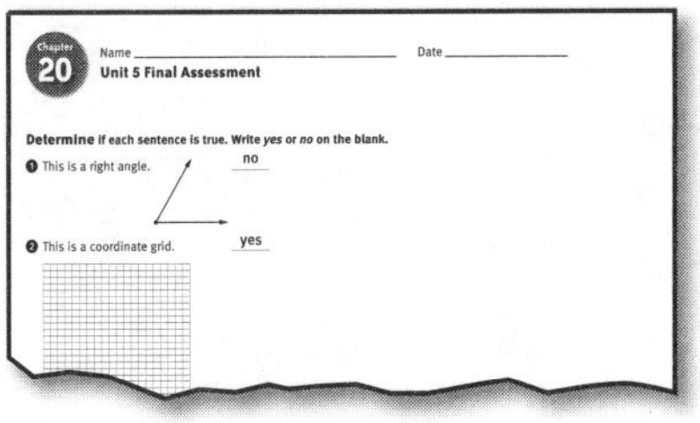

Chapter 20 Name Date
Unit 5 Final Assessment

Determine if each sentence is true. Write *yes* or *no* on the blank.

1 This is a right angle. no

2 This is a coordinate grid. yes

Final Assessment, p. 91

- **Beginning English Learners:** 0–2 of Questions 1–6 correct
- **Intermediate English Learners:** 3–4 of Questions 1–6 correct
- **Advanced English Learners:** 5–6 of Questions 1–6 correct

Use the Student Assessment Record, page 144, to record the assessment results.

Name ______________________ Date ______________

Practice 1

Determine if each angle is a right angle. Write *yes* or *no* on the blank.

❶ 

____

❸ 

____

❷ 

____

Determine if each sentence is true. Write *yes* or *no* on the blank.

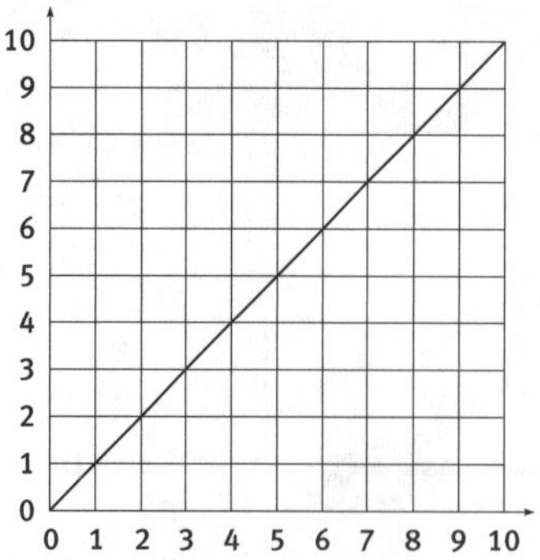

❹ This is a coordinate grid. ____________

❺ The line has slope. ____________

Chapter 20

Name ______________________ Date ____________

Practice 2

Ask your classmates the following questions. Have a different person answer each question. Write your answers in complete sentences. Be ready to share your answers with the class.

1. Who can find a right angle? What is a right angle?

2. Who can find a hypotenuse? What is a hypotenuse?

3. Who can point to a vertical line? What is a vertical line?

4. Who can point to a horizontal line? What is a horizontal line?

5. Who can describe the Pythagorean theorem? What does the Pythagorean theorem state?

6. Who can give an example of a rate? What is a rate?

Chapter 20

Name ______________________ Date ______________

Practice 3

Read each sentence below, and follow the directions carefully.

1. Draw a coordinate grid below and label the x-axis and the y-axis.

2. Look at the equation $2x + 1 = y$. If $x = 2$, what does y equal? Write the answer. ____________

3. If $x = 4$, what does y equal? Write the answer. ____________

4. What are the ordered pairs for $x = 2$ and $x = 4$? ______________

5. Plot the ordered pairs on the coordinate grid, and connect them with a line.

6. Draw a horizontal line on the coordinate grid.

Chapter 20

Name ______________________ Date ______________

Unit 5 Final Assessment

Determine if each sentence is true. Write *yes* or *no* on the blank.

1. This is a right angle. ______

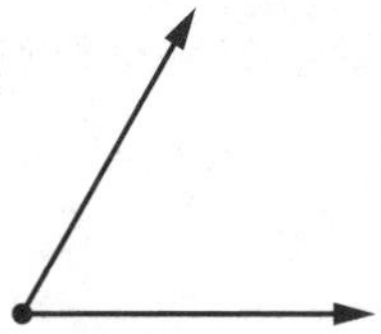

2. This is a coordinate grid. ______

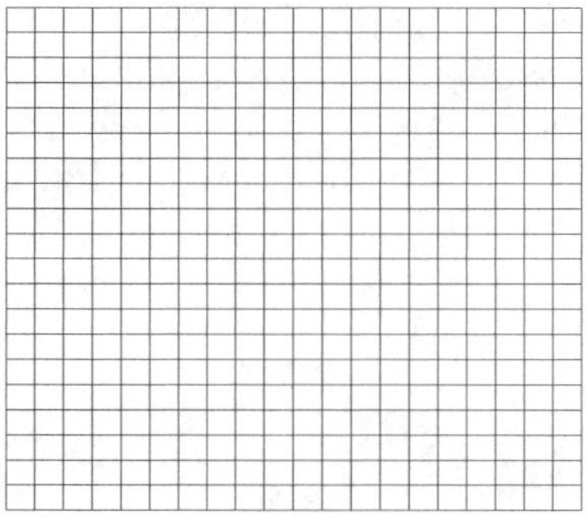

Follow the directions.

3. Label the *x*-axis and *y*-axis.

4. Draw a horizontal line, a vertical line, and a line with slope on the grid.

   Label each line *H*, *V*, or *S*.

5. Label the hypotenuse of the triangle below.

6. Write the length of the hypotenuse. __________

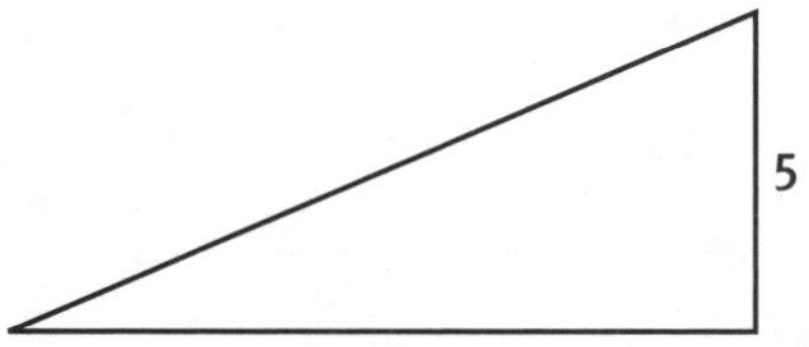

Algebra

Unit at a Glance

In this unit, students will learn the vocabulary associated with ***Number Worlds,*** Algebra Readiness, Algebra. In this unit, students will learn how to use the distributive property; evaluate expressions using roots and exponents; understand the Pythagorean theorem; simplify expressions involving exponents; and solve problems with one variable. Before beginning the unit, assess students' general knowledge of math and vocabulary using the Individual Oral Assessment on page 93.

How Students Learn Vocabulary

Using visuals and manipulatives creates familiarity for English learners and has an immediate impact on learning language. For this unit, it will be helpful to have Magnetic Number Lines and Chips, pattern blocks, fraction circles, geoboards, Counters, and attribute blocks on hand so students can visualize the reality of the operations they will be conducting. Having students create their own examples of new vocabulary is another useful way to connect students to the reality of what they are learning.

Academic Vocabulary Taught in Unit 6

Chapter 21	Chapter 22	Chapter 23	Chapter 24
distributive property The product of multiplication is the same when the operation is performed on the whole set as when it is performed on the individual members of the set **exponent** A numeral or symbol placed at the upper right side of another numeral or symbol to indicate the number of times it is to be multiplied by itself **opposite** A number that can be added to the original number and result in zero **reciprocal** One of two quantities whose product is 1 **square root** The factor of a number that when multiplied by itself gives the number	**Pythagorean theorem** Named for the Greek mathematician Pythagoras; for any right triangle, the square of the length of the hypotenuse is equal to the sum of the squares of the lengths of the other two sides; written as $a^2 + b^2 = c^2$, where c is the length of the hypotenuse, and *a* and *b* are the lengths of the other sides **unknown** A variable that is a solution to an equation	**linear function** The relationship between two quantities which shows an increase or decrease at a constant rate **operation** Something done to one or more numbers or algebraic expressions; addition, subtraction, multiplication, and division are the four most common operations **order of operations** The agreed-upon operational priority for problems containing more than one operation **variable** A symbol that represents a quantity	**inequality** A number sentence stating that two quantities are not equal. Relation symbols for inequalities include $<$ (less than), and $>$ (greater than) **graph** A diagram showing the relationship between two or more sets of data **greater than** Larger in number or measure **less than** Smaller in number or measure

Unit 6 Individual Oral Assessment

Directions: Read each question to the student, and record his or her oral responses. Some questions have teacher directions. Teacher directions are indicated in italics. Allow students to use pencil and paper to work their responses.

1. Is this a **graph**? *Show student a coordinate grid.* yes
2. Is this an **inequality**? *Write* $x + 2 = 5y$ *on a piece of paper.* no
3. Is this the **reciprocal** of 4? *Write* $\frac{1}{4}$ *on a piece of paper.* yes
4. What is the **square root** of 100? 10
5. What number is the **opposite** of negative three? 3 or positive 3
6. Which number is the **exponent**? *Write* 4^5 *on a piece of paper.* 5
7. Which number is **greater than** 15? *Write* 12 *and* 20 *on a piece of paper.* 20
8. Is this a **linear function** or an **inequality**? *Write* $3(x + 1) = y$ *on a piece of paper.* linear function
9. What are the **variables**? *Show student the same linear function.* x and y
10. What does the **unknown** equal? *Show student a right triangle with the hypotenuse labeled x and sides labeled* 6 *and* 8. $6^2 + 8^2$
11. What is the value of the **unknown**? *Show student the same right triangle.* 10
12. Describe how to use the **distributive property** to solve 43×5. Student should describe multiplying 40 by 5 (200), multiplying 3 by 5 (15), and adding 200 and 15 together to arrive at an answer of 215.
13. What is the **reciprocal** of $\frac{3}{4}$? $\frac{4}{3}$

- **Beginning English Learners:** 0–3 of questions 1–10 correct
- **Intermediate English Learners:** 4–7 of questions 1–10 correct
- **Advanced English Learners:** 8–10 of questions 1–10 correct
- If the student is able to answer Questions 11–13, then he or she can understand the mathematics taught in this unit, but may still have difficulty with the academic vocabulary.

Use the Student Assessment Record, page 144, to record the assessment results.

Unit 6 • Algebra

Objective

Students can understand the meanings of the terms ***exponent, opposite, reciprocal, distributive,*** and ***square root.***

Materials

Program Materials

- Vocabulary Cards 11 (exponent), 37 (reciprocal), and 44 (square root)
- You Are My Match If..., p. 133
- Magnetic Number Line and Chips 

Additional Materials

Scissors

Vocabulary

distributive property The product of multiplication is the same when the operation is performed on the whole set as when it is performed on the individual members of the set

exponent A numeral or symbol placed at the upper right side of another numeral or symbol to indicate the number of times it is to be multiplied by itself

opposite A number that can be added to the original number and result in zero

reciprocal One of two quantities whose product is 1

square root The factor of a number that when multiplied by itself gives the number

1 Warm Up

Introduce each vocabulary word to students.
Say the word aloud.
Have students repeat the word.

After students have listened to the words, show them ***Vocabulary Cards* 11, 37,** and **44.**

Distribute a Magnetic Number Line and Chips to each student. Have students label the Magnetic Number Line with zero at the middle hatch mark, positive numbers extending to the right, and negative numbers extending to the left. Have students put a Chip on the number 8 on the Magnetic Number Line.

- **What is the opposite of the number 8?** −8

Tell students that when opposite numbers are added together, they result in zero. Say *opposite*, and have students repeat the word. Write *opposite* on the board.

- **Does this remind you of anything you have already learned?** Students may remember the vocabulary word *inverse* from Unit 3.

Write $\frac{3}{4}$ on the board. Next to it, write $\frac{4}{3}$. Ask students what they notice about these numbers. Tell them that fractions are reciprocal if their product is 1 when they are multiplied. Say *reciprocal*, and have students repeat the word. Write *reciprocal* on the board.

- **Does this remind you of anything you have already learned?** Students may remember the vocabulary word *reciprocal* from Unit 3.

2 Engage

Write $43 \times 6 = ?$ on the board.

Then, write it another way: $(40 \times 6) + (3 \times 6) = ?$

Have students solve both problems.

- **Is the answer to both problems the same?** yes
- **What is the answer?** 258

Tell students they can use this distributive property to help them solve more difficult multiplication operations. Say *distributive property*, and have students repeat the term. Write *distributive property* on the board.

Show students a checkerboard and discuss what it is.

- **Is it a square?** yes
- **How many little squares are on this board?** 64

On the board, show students that instead of adding $8 + 8 + 8 + 8 + 8 + 8 + 8 + 8$, they can also multiply 8×8 to arrive at the same answer, 64. Because they are multiplying a number by itself, it can also be written as 8^2, or 8 squared. The 8 is called the base, and the superscript 2 is called the exponent. Say *exponent*, and have students repeat the word. Write *exponent* on the board.

The square root of 64 is 8. *Say square root*, and have students repeat the term. Write *square root* on the board.

Organize students into small groups. Distribute a copy of You Are My Match If..., p. 133, and a pair of scissors to each student. Have students cut out the cards from the worksheet, and play a few rounds of the game with their group. Monitor the groups to make sure students are making proper requests of the other players. For example, if a student has *The reciprocal of 7* in her hand, she would say, "You are my match if you have $\frac{1}{7}$."

Teacher's Note

To save time, prepare ahead several decks of cards for the You Are My Match If... game. You may also want to have students look over the cards and find the matches prior to playing the game so they feel comfortable with what words they will be saying.

Progress Monitoring

If . . .	Then . . .
If . . . students struggle to determine the reciprocal of the number 7,	**Then . . .** show them how the number can be written as the fraction $\frac{7}{1}$.

3 Reflect

Extended Response

- **What is a reciprocal?**
- **What is the difference between a reciprocal and an opposite?**
- **What is an exponent?**
- **What is one reason why exponents might be used?**

Encourage student discussion of these questions and answers.

Progress Monitoring

If . . .	Then . . .
If . . . students are having trouble with the lesson vocabulary,	**Then . . .** review with them individually.

4 Assess

Informal Assessment

Have students complete the activity below to make sure they understand the vocabulary. As students use each word:

1. Check understanding.
2. Correct errors.
3. Recheck for understanding.

- Have students explain the difference between an opposite and a reciprocal.
- Have students explain the distributive property and give an example of it.
- Have students explain how exponents and square roots are related.

For each word, use the following rubric to assign a score.

The student can repeat the word when prompted. (1 point)

The student knows the word but does not know its meaning. (2 points)

The student has a vague idea of the word's meaning. (3 points)

The student knows the word and can use the word in context. (4 points)

Chapter 22

Unit 6 • Algebra

Objective

Students can understand the meanings of the terms *unknown* and *Pythagorean theorem.*

Materials

Program Materials

Vocabulary Card 31 (Pythagorean theorem)

Additional Materials

- Pattern blocks
- Attribute blocks
- Fraction circles
- Geoboards
- Graph paper

Vocabulary

Pythagorean theorem Named for the Greek mathematician Pythagoras; for any right triangle, the square of the length of the hypotenuse is equal to the sum of the squares of the lengths of the other two sides; written as $a^2 + b^2 = c^2$, where c is the length of the hypotenuse, and a and b are the lengths of the other sides

unknown A variable that is a solution to an equation

1 Warm Up

Introduce each vocabulary word to students. Say the word aloud. Have students repeat the word.

After students have listened to the words, show them ***Vocabulary Card 31.***

Organize students into pairs. Distribute a handful of pattern blocks, attribute blocks, fraction circles, or a mix of all three to each pair of students. Have them identify any of the shapes that have at least one right angle. Ask students if any of the shapes are right triangles.

Distribute a geoboard or graph paper to each pair of students. Have students create a right triangle on a geoboard or on graph paper.

2 Engage

Have students look at the right triangles they created and point to the side opposite the right angle.

- **What is this side called?** the hypotenuse
- **How many units long is one of the other sides?** Answers will vary, but will represent the triangles the students created.
- **How many units long is the third side?** Answers will vary, but will represent the triangles the students created.

Draw on the board a right triangle according to one student's measurements for the triangle sides; for example, 3 and 4. Label the sides, and then label the hypotenuse as x.

Tell students that we do not know the value of x, so it is an unknown. Say *unknown*, and have students repeat the word. Write *unknown* on the board.

Write x = ? on the board.

- **What does the unknown, x, equal?** x = the square root of $3^2 + 4^2$
- **What is this called?** the Pythagorean theorem

Say *Pythagorean theorem*, and have students repeat the term. Write *Pythagorean theorem* on the board.

Have students close their eyes and listen carefully as you tell the following story.

Elizabeth and Clara go to the same school. Elizabeth lives eight miles north of the school, and Clara lives six miles west of the school. How far apart do Elizabeth and Clara live?

After you have told the story one time, have students create a map on a piece of graph paper as you tell the story again. Suggest that students start by marking the location of the school and then the two homes. Guide students to see that they will use the Pythagorean theorem to solve this story problem. The answer to the problem is ten miles.

Teacher's Note

Give students ample opportunities to practice saying *Pythagorean theorem*. The /th/ sound does not exist in many languages, so it may be difficult for some students to pronounce. Praise them for any attempts they make.

Progress Monitoring

If . . .	Then . . .
If . . . students are confused about which side of a triangle is the hypotenuse,	**Then . . .** remind them that the hypotenuse is the side that does not form the right angle.

3 Reflect

Extended Response

- **What is the hypotenuse in the story problem? How do you know?**
- **Was the story problem activity difficult for you? Why or why not?**
- **What rule did you have to use to solve the story problem?**
- **Describe how you solved the story problem.**

Encourage student discussion of these questions and answers.

Progress Monitoring

If . . .	Then . . .
If . . . students struggle to follow the story problem,	**Then . . .** slow down and repeat the story as necessary, and allow students to help each other by explaining, in English, the steps involved for creating an equation and solving for the unknown.

4 Assess

Informal Assessment

Have students complete the activity below to make sure they understand the vocabulary. As students use each word:

1. Check understanding.
2. Correct errors.
3. Recheck for understanding.

Have students describe the Pythagorean theorem and how they use the Pythagorean theorem to solve for an unknown length in a triangle.

For each word, use the following rubric to assign a score.

The student can repeat the word when prompted. (1 point)

The student knows the word but does not know its meaning. (2 points)

The student has a vague idea of the word's meaning. (3 points)

The student knows the word and can use the word in context. (4 points)

Objective

Students can review the meaning of the term *variable* and can understand the meanings of the terms *operation*, *order of operations*, and *linear function.*

Materials

Program Materials

- Vocabulary Card 49 (variable)
- Linear Equations and Variables, p. 134

Additional Materials

Graph paper

Vocabulary

linear function The relationship between two quantities which shows an increase or decrease at a constant rate

operation Something done to one or more numbers or algebraic expressions; addition, subtraction, multiplication, and division are the four most common operations

order of operations The agreed-upon operational priority for problems containing more than one operation

variable A symbol that represents a quantity

1 Warm Up

Introduce each vocabulary word to students.
Say the word aloud.
Have students repeat the word.

After students have listened to the words, show them ***Vocabulary Card 49.***

Review previously learned vocabulary. Write the following function on the board: $2x + 1 = y$. Circle the function.

- **What is this called?** function

Circle the *x*.

- **What is this called?** variable

Circle the *y*.

- **What is this called?** variable

Point to the 2.

- **What is this called?** constant

- **To solve this function, do we add, subtract, multiply, and/or divide?** add and multiply

Tell students that addition, subtraction, multiplication, and division are called operations. Say *operations*, and have students repeat the word. Write *operations* on the board.

2 Engage

Return to the function $2x + 1 = y$.

- **How many operations do we need to do in this function?** 2
- **What are they?** multiplication and addition
- **What do we multiply?** 2 and *x*
- **What do we add?** 2*x* and 1
- **Do we add or multiply first?** multiply

Tell students that the order of operations in a function is very important. Say *order of operations,* and have students repeat the term. Write *order of operations* on the board.

Distribute graph paper to each student.

- **If we substitute the value of 1 for x, what is the value of y?** 3
- **So, if $x = 1$ and $y = 3$, what is the ordered pair?** (1, 3)

Repeat for x-values of 2, 3, 4, and 5. Plot the points on a coordinate grid on the board or overhead transparency. Have students plot the same points on graph paper. Point out how plotted points can be connected with a straight line. Because of this, the function is also called a linear equation. Say *linear equation,* and have students repeat the term. Write *linear equation* on the board.

Organize students into pairs. Distribute a copy of Linear Equations and Variables, p. 134, to each student. Have students complete the worksheet and compare answers with a partner. Monitor and give feedback.

Write the following scenario on the board or overhead transparency.

Sara receives $5 spending money each week. If Sara saves half of her money, how much will she have after 4 weeks?

Have students work with their partner to determine the answer, and then ask them to write and graph a linear equation to show Sara's savings over time. Have students determine the variables.

Teacher's Note

English learners know the word *graph* but may find it confusing when the word is used as a verb. Point out that context is important, and when *graph* is preceded by an article (*a, the,* or *this*), it is a noun. When *graph* is preceded by *to* it is a verb.

Progress Monitoring

If . . .	Then . . .
If . . . students have trouble understanding the vocabulary,	**Then . . .** work with them independently on concepts and pronunciation.

3 Reflect

Extended Response

- **Why is order of operations important?**
- **How do we use linear equations every day?**
- **Can you think of a reason to write a linear equation?**

Encourage student discussion of these questions and answers.

Progress Monitoring

If . . .	Then . . .
If . . . students seem slow to participate in the Extended Response activity,	**Then . . .** allow them a little extra time to formulate their answers, or conduct the activity in pairs or small groups to maximize speaking opportunities.

4 Assess

Informal Assessment

Have students complete the activity below to make sure they understand the vocabulary. As students use each word:

1. Check understanding.
2. Correct errors.
3. Recheck for understanding.

- Have students name operations and explain why the order of operations is important.
- Have students define *linear equation* in their own words.

For each word, use the followin g rubric to assign a score.

The Student can repeat the word when prompted. (1 point)

The student knows the word but does not know its meaning. (2 points)

The student has a vague idea of the word's meaning. (3 points)

The student knows the word and can use the word in context. (4 points)

Chapter 24

Unit 6 • Algebra

Objective

Students can understand the meanings of the terms *less than*, *greater than*, *inequality*, and *graph.*

Materials

Program Materials

- Two-Color Counters

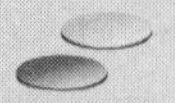

- Magnetic Number Lines

Vocabulary

inequality A number sentence stating that two quantities are not equal. Relation symbols for inequalities include < (less than), and > (greater than)

graph A diagram showing the relationship between two or more sets of data

greater than Larger in number or measure

less than Smaller in number or measure

1 Warm Up

Introduce each vocabulary word to students.
Say the word aloud.
Have students repeat the word.

Have each student take a handful of Counters and count them. Have students practice any vocabulary they have learned so far this year, including division and multiplication vocabulary, size and shape vocabulary, and exponent vocabulary.

2 Engage

Ask one student:

- **How many Counters do you have?**

Then ask another student:

- **Is your number of Counters higher or lower than that?**

Consider the example that Student A has 12 Counters and Student B has 15 Counters. Explain that when a number is higher than another number, we say it is greater than that number. Say *greater than,* and have students repeat the term. Write 15 is *greater than* 12 on the board. Then write the same sentence using the mathematical symbol >: 15 > 12.

Repeat for *less than.*

Now give each student a unique number of Counters. Conduct a guessing game. Begin the game by asking one student:

- **Is your number of Counters greater (or less) than 4?**

Write the question on the board after the answer is given. Have students take turns asking greater than/ less than questions until they can guess exactly how many Counters each student has.

When the activity is completed, write an inequality sentence on the board; for example, *Kenji's number is greater than five.* Next to the sentence write K > 5. Tell students that this is called an inequality, because the two sides are not equal. Say *inequality,* and have students repeat the word. Write *inequality* on the board. Continue with other examples of inequalities until students are firm in their understanding.

Show students a coordinate grid on an overhead transparency. Tell them that the grid can also be called a graph. Say *graph,* and have students repeat the word. Write *graph* on the board.

Show students how to graph the idea of inequality. For example, to graph y < 5, shade all the area below 5 on the y-axis. For every value of x, all values of y that are less than 5 will be shaded. Repeat for x > 3. Then show them how the overlapping area on the graph represents y < 5 <u>and</u> x > 3.

Teacher's Note

Students may need additional practice with inequalities. If students need another visual reference for inequalities, organize students into pairs. Distribute a Magnetic Number Line and Chips to each pair of students and have students place Chips according to their partner's verbal description. For example, one student may say "Put a Chip on a number that is less than 2," and the other student may place a Chip on –3.

Using Student Worksheets

After students complete the activity, help them complete the appropriate Practice for their levels of English development.

Level 1, Practice 1, p. 102

Level 2, Practice 2, p. 103

Level 3, Practice 3, p. 104

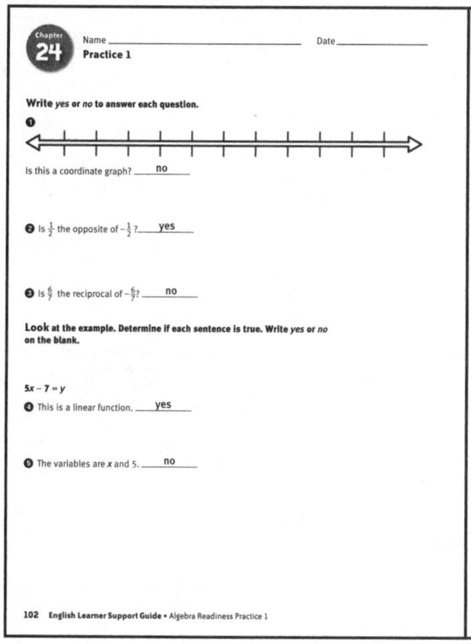
Chapter 24
Name ________ Date ________
Practice 1

Write *yes* or *no* to answer each question.

1. Is this a coordinate graph? no

2. Is $\frac{1}{2}$ the opposite of $-\frac{1}{2}$? yes

3. Is $\frac{6}{7}$ the reciprocal of $-\frac{6}{7}$? no

Look at the example. Determine if each sentence is true. Write *yes* or *no* on the blank.

$5x - 7 = y$

4. This is a linear function. yes

5. The variables are x and 5. no

102 English Learner Support Guide • Algebra Readiness Practice 1

Practice 1, p. 102

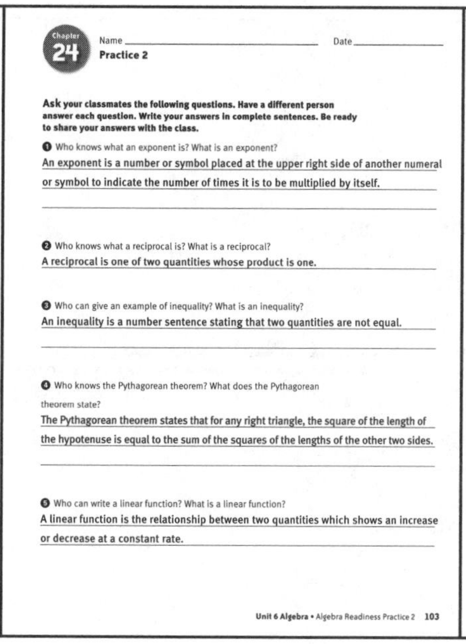
Chapter 24
Name ________ Date ________
Practice 2

Ask your classmates the following questions. Have a different person answer each question. Write your answers in complete sentences. Be ready to share your answers with the class.

1. Who knows what an exponent is? What is an exponent?
An exponent is a number or symbol placed at the upper right side of another numeral or symbol to indicate the number of times it is to be multiplied by itself.

2. Who knows what a reciprocal is? What is a reciprocal?
A reciprocal is one of two quantities whose product is one.

3. Who can give an example of inequality? What is an inequality?
An inequality is a number sentence stating that two quantities are not equal.

4. Who knows the Pythagorean theorem? What does the Pythagorean theorem state?
The Pythagorean theorem states that for any right triangle, the square of the length of the hypotenuse is equal to the sum of the squares of the lengths of the other two sides.

5. Who can write a linear function? What is a linear function?
A linear function is the relationship between two quantities which shows an increase or decrease at a constant rate.

Unit 6 Algebra • Algebra Readiness Practice 2 103

Practice 2, p. 103

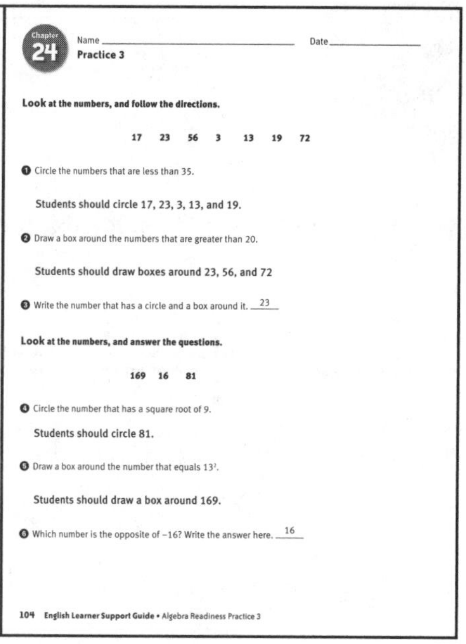
Chapter 24
Name ________ Date ________
Practice 3

Look at the numbers, and follow the directions.

17 23 56 3 13 19 72

1. Circle the numbers that are less than 35.
Students should circle 17, 23, 3, 13, and 19.

2. Draw a box around the numbers that are greater than 20.
Students should draw boxes around 23, 56, and 72

3. Write the number that has a circle and a box around it. 23

Look at the numbers, and answer the questions.

169 16 81

4. Circle the number that has a square root of 9.
Students should circle 81.

5. Draw a box around the number that equals 13^2.
Students should draw a box around 169.

6. Which number is the opposite of −16? Write the answer here. 16

104 English Learner Support Guide • Algebra Readiness Practice 3

Practice 3, p. 104

3 Reflect

Extended Response

- **How are graphs helpful?**
- **What is an inequality?**
- **Give an example of things that are not equal.**

Encourage student discussion of these questions and answers.

4 Assess

Informal Assessment

Have students complete the following activity to make sure they understand the vocabulary. As students use each word:

1. Check understanding.
2. Correct errors.
3. Recheck for understanding.

- Have students compare numbers using the terms *greater than* and *less than*.
- Have students explain how to graph an inequality.

For each word, use the following rubric to assign a score.

The student can repeat the word when prompted. (1 point)

The student knows the word but does not know its meaning. (2 points)

The student has a vague idea of the word's meaning. (3 points)

The student knows the word and can use the word in context. (4 points)

Final Assessment

Distribute a copy of the Final Assessment, p. 105, to each student. Use the following rubric to determine each student's level of English development.

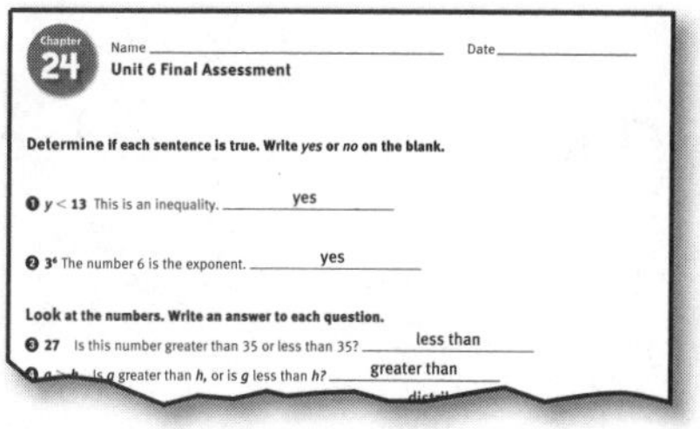
Chapter 24
Name ________ Date ________
Unit 6 Final Assessment

Determine if each sentence is true. Write *yes* or *no* on the blank.

1. $y < 13$ This is an inequality. yes

2. 3^6 The number 6 is the exponent. yes

Look at the numbers. Write an answer to each question.

3. 27 Is this number greater than 35 or less than 35? less than

4. $g > h$ Is g greater than h, or is g less than h? greater than

Final Assessment, p. 105

- **Beginning English Learners:** 0–2 of Questions 1–6 correct
- **Intermediate English Learners:** 3–4 of Questions 1–6 correct
- **Advanced English Learners:** 5–6 of Questions 1–6 correct

Use the Student Assessment Record, page 144, to record the assessment results.

Chapter 24

Name ____________________ Date ____________

Practice 1

Write *yes* or *no* to answer each question.

1. 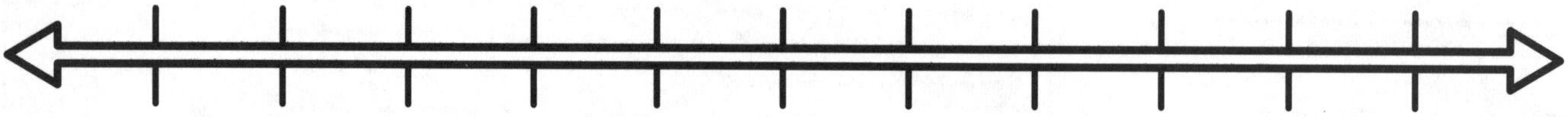

Is this a coordinate graph? ____________

2. Is $\frac{1}{2}$ the opposite of $-\frac{1}{2}$? ____________

3. Is $\frac{6}{7}$ the reciprocal of $-\frac{6}{7}$? ____________

Look at the example. Determine if each sentence is true. Write *yes* or *no* on the blank.

$5x - 7 = y$

4. This is a linear function. ____________

5. The variables are x and 5. ____________

Chapter 24

Name ______________________ Date ____________

Practice 2

Ask your classmates the following questions. Have a different person answer each question. Write your answers in complete sentences. Be ready to share your answers with the class.

1. Who knows what an exponent is? What is an exponent?

____

____

____

2. Who knows what a reciprocal is? What is a reciprocal?

____

3. Who can give an example of inequality? What is an inequality?

____

____

4. Who knows the Pythagorean theorem? What does the Pythagorean theorem state?

____

____

____

5. Who can write a linear function? What is a linear function?

____

____

Name ______________________________ Date ______________

Practice 3

Look at the numbers, and follow the directions.

17 23 56 3 13 19 72

1. Circle the numbers that are less than 35.

2. Draw a box around the numbers that are greater than 20.

3. Write the number that has a circle and a box around it. ______

Look at the numbers, and answer the questions.

169 16 81

4. Circle the number that has a square root of 9.

5. Draw a box around the number that equals 13^2.

6. Which number is the opposite of -16? Write the answer here. ______

Chapter 24

Name ______________________ Date ______________

Unit 6 Final Assessment

Determine if each sentence is true. Write *yes* or *no* on the blank.

❶ $y < 13$ This is an inequality. ______________

❷ 3^6 The number 6 is the exponent. ______________

Look at the numbers. Write an answer to each question.

❸ **27** Is this number greater than 35 or less than 35? ______________

❹ $g > h$ Is *g* greater than *h*, or is *g* less than *h*? ______________

❺ $43 \times 5 = (40 \times 5) + (3 \times 5)$ What property is this? ______________

❻ $a^2 + b^2 = c^2$ What is this called? ______________

Vocabulary Cards

Blackline masters of the words included on the ***SRA Math Vocabulary Cards*** are included for reproduction on the following pages. Use them as suggested, or create your own variations, to enhance vocabulary development.

- **Flash Cards** Make flash cards with words on one side of the card and definitions on the other side.
- **Resource Cards** Make resource cards with the definitions, or an illustration, on the same side of the card as the word.
- **Matching** Match the words with their definitions, written on additional cards.
- **Matching Pairs** Place cards in columns and rows facedown, turning two cards over at a time to match word pairs.
- **Organize** Use graphic organizers to group words into categories.
- **Bingo** Use words students have studied. Call out definitions. Have students cover the words with counters until they get four or five words in a row.
- **Picture Cards** Create an illustration of the word as a visual reference.

acute angle

area

circumference

complementary angles

congruent

decimal

degree

diameter

divide

equivalent fractions

exponent

fraction

function

hypotenuse

integer

intersecting lines

	line segment
	mean
	multiply
	mixed number

negative number

obtuse angle

ordered pair

parallelogram

	percent
	perimeter
	polygon
	prime number

prism

product

Pythagorean theorem

quadrilateral

	quotient
	radius
	range
	ratio

reciprocal

reflection

right angle

rotation

scale

similar

slope

square root

supplementary angles

symmetry

translation

triangle

variable

volume

Answers

Unit 1, Practice 1, p. 32

1. no 2. no 3. yes
4. yes 5. no 6. yes

Unit 1, Practice 2, p. 33

1. The number 4 is the divisor.
2. The number 286 is the dividend.
3. The number 2 is the remainder.
4. The quotient is 71 R 2.
5. The product is 741.
6. The factors are 247 and 3.
7. There are three digits in the product.
8. There are three digits in 247 and 1 digit in 3.

Unit 1, Practice 3, p. 34

1. Students should circle 87.
2. Students should draw a triangle around the 29 in the division problem.
3. Students should draw a box around 20 R 1.
4. Students should draw a star next to 1.
5. 29; 3
6. Students should underline all digits in the ones place.

Unit 1, Final Assessment, p. 35

1. yes 2. no 3. 7
4. 4 5. 3,600 6. 1

Unit 2, Practice 1, p. 46

1. yes 2. no 3. yes
4. yes 5. yes

Unit 2, Practice 2, p. 47

1. An integer is any positive or negative whole number or zero.
2. A negative number is a number that is less than zero.
3. The base is 2 and the exponent is 5. An exponent is a numeral or symbol placed at the upper right side of another numeral or symbol to indicate the number of times it is to be multiplied by itself.
4. A prime number is a whole number that has only two factors, the number itself and 1. The prime numbers to 50 are 2, 3, 5, 7, 11, 13, 17, 19, 23, 29, 31, 37, 41, 43, and 47.
5. An equivalent fraction is a fraction that names the same rational number. A fraction that is equivalent to $\frac{4}{6}$ is $\frac{8}{12}$.
6. A percent is a special fraction with a denominator of 100. A percent that equals $\frac{8}{10}$ is 80%.

Unit 2, Practice 3, p. 48

1. 2^4 2. $1\frac{1}{4}$
3. Students should circle $\frac{1}{5}$.
4. Students should draw a box around 6.
5. 0.80
6. Negative numbers are numbers that are less than zero.

Unit 2, Final Assessment, p. 49

1. yes 2. no 3. numerator
4. prime 5. 0.50; 50% 6. $\frac{7}{8}$; 87.5%

Unit 3, Practice 1, p. 60

1. Students should circle 5.
2. Students should circle 9.7.
3. yes 4. yes 5. no

Unit 3, Practice 2, p. 61

1. No, these numbers are not equal.
2. Yes, this is a rational number.
3. These numbers are reciprocal.
4. An equivalent percent for this fraction is 62.5%.
5. The additive inverse is −25.
6. The number 15 is the numerator.

Unit 3, Practice 3, p. 62

1. Students should write a 3 as the numerator.
2. Students should write a 4 as the denominator.
3. 0.75 4. 75% 5. no
6. yes 7. $\frac{4}{3}$ 8. 12

Unit 3, Final Assessment, p. 63

1. no 2. yes 3. yes

4. $\frac{4}{3}$ 5. 4 and 9 6. 4

Unit 4, Practice 1, p. 74

1. yes 2. no 3. yes

4. yes 5. yes 6. no

Unit 4, Practice 2, p. 75

1. The numbers 3 and 5 are constants.
2. The variables are x and y.
3. If x equals 3, y equals 45.
4. The symbols around $x \times 3$ are called parentheses.
5. This is the commutative property of multiplication.
6. This is the associative property of multiplication.

Unit 4, Practice 3, p. 76

1. Students should circle 2 and 1.
2. Students should draw boxes around x and y.
3. 1; 2; 3; 4; 5 4. $(2 + x) + 1 = y$
5. Possible answer: $x + 2 + 1 = y$.

Unit 4, Final Assessment, p. 77

1. yes 2. no 3. yes

4. 90 5. 120 6. 150

Unit 5, Practice 1, p. 88

1. yes 2. no 3. no

4. yes 5. yes

Unit 5, Practice 2, p. 89

1. A right angle is an angle measuring 90 degrees.
2. A hypotenuse is the side of a right triangle opposite the right angle.
3. A vertical line is a line that is perpendicular to the horizon.
4. A horizontal line is a line that is parallel to the horizon.
5. The Pythagorean theorem states that for any right triangle, the square of the length of the hypotenuse is equal to the sum of the squares of the lengths of the other two sides.
6. A rate is a ratio comparing two quantities with unlike units.

Unit 5, Practice 3, p. 90

1., 5., 6. Students should draw and label the x-axis and the y-axis, plot the points (2, 5) and (4, 9) and connect them with a line, and draw a horizontal line on the cooordinate grid.

2. $y = 5$ 3. $y = 9$ 4. (2, 5) and (4, 9)

Unit 5, Final Assessment, p. 91

1. no 2. yes

3. Students should label the x-axis and the y-axis.
4. Students should draw a horizontal line labeled H, a vertical line labeled V, and a line with slope labeled S on the grid.
5. Students should label the hypotenuse. 6. 13

Unit 6, Practice 1, p. 102

1. no 2. yes 3. no

4. yes 5. no

Unit 6, Practice 2, p. 103

1. An exponent is a number or symbol placed at the upper right side of another numeral or symbol to indicate the number of times it is to be multiplied by itself.
2. A reciprocal is one of two quantities whose product is one.
3. An inequality is a number sentence stating that two quantities are not equal.
4. The Pythagorean theorem states that for any right triangle, the square of the length of the hypotenuse is equal to the sum of the squares of the lengths of the other two sides.
5. A linear function is the relationship between two quantities which shows an increase or decrease at a constant rate.

Unit 6, Practice 3, p. 104

1. Students should circle 17, 23, 3, 13, and 19.
2. Students should draw boxes around 23, 56, and 72.
3. 23 4. Students should circle 81.
5. Students should draw a box around 169.
6. 16

Answers

Unit 6, Final Assessment, p. 105

1. yes 2. yes
3. less than 4. greater than
5. distributive 6. Pythagorean theorem

Place Value, p. 123

1. hundreds 2. thousands 3. ones
4. tens 5. tens 6. thousands
7. tens 8. ones 9. thousands
10. hundreds 11. less than
12. greater than 13. less than
14. less than

Divide and Conquer, p. 124

1. dividend; divisor; quotient; 3
2. no remainder; quotient; divisor; dividend
3. dividend; 7; quotient; divisor
4. divisor; dividend; quotient no remainder

Fractions and Decimals, p. 125

1. decimal number
2. fraction or denominator
3. fraction or denominator
4. numerator
5. B 6. C 7. A 8. D

Percents and Their Equivalents, p. 126

1. no 2. yes

0.20; $\frac{1}{2}$; 50%; 0.625; $\frac{7}{20}$; 0.35; $\frac{7}{10}$; 70%

Addition Vocabulary and Ratios, p.127

1. addend 2. addend 3. sum
4. addend 5. sum 6. addend
7. addend 8. sum 9. addend
10. sum 11. addition 12. both
13. ratio 14. addition

Reciprocals and Inverses, p. 128

1. $\frac{5}{4}$; $-\frac{4}{5}$ 2. $\frac{1}{92}$; -92 3. $-\frac{4}{3}$; $\frac{3}{4}$
4. $\frac{1}{150}$; -150 5. $-\frac{13}{9}$; $\frac{9}{13}$ 6. $\frac{1}{6}$; 6
7. $\frac{1}{22}$; -22 8. $-\frac{1}{8}$; 8
9. $\frac{6}{5}$; $-\frac{5}{6}$ 10. $\frac{1}{3}$; -3

Expressions and Equations, p. 129

1. expression 2. expression 3. equation
4. equation 5. expression 6. 7

Evaluate the Expression, p. 129

7. 15 8. 3 9. 33 10. 0

Function Tables, p. 130

10¢; 20¢; 30¢; 40¢; 60¢; 70¢; 80¢

$x \times 25¢ = y$

25¢; 50¢; 75¢; 100¢; 125¢; 150¢; 175¢; 200¢

Graphing Variables, p. 131

7¢; 14¢; 21¢; 28¢; 42¢; 49¢; 56¢

(1, 7); (2, 14); (3, 21); (4, 28); (6, 42); (7, 49); (8, 56)

Vertical, Horizontal, or Slope? p. 132

2. Answers will vary, but should match the x-values for the vertical line.
3. Answers will vary, but should match the y-values for the horizontal line.
4. (−4, −2), (−2, 0), (0, 2), (2, 4)

Linear Equations and Variables, p. 134

1. *x* and *y*; yes 2. *x* and *y*; no
3. *a*, *b*, and *c*; no 4. *x* and *y*; yes
5. *m*; yes

Name ______________________ Date ______________

Place Value

Look at the underlined number. What is the place value? Write *thousands, hundreds, tens*, or *ones*.

1. $4,\underline{7}90$ ____________
2. $\underline{7},932$ ____________
3. $47\underline{3}$ ____________
4. $6,5\underline{7}2$ ____________
5. $9,8\underline{6}2$ ____________
6. $\underline{9},365$ ____________
7. $3,5\underline{0}2$ ____________
8. $5,90\underline{3}$ ____________
9. $\underline{4},112$ ____________
10. $6,\underline{7}85$ ____________

Write *greater than* or *less than*.

11. 535 is ____________ 622.
12. 1,522 is ____________ 1,499.
13. 4,809 is ____________ 6,227.
14. 92 is ____________ 142.

Name ______________________ Date ______________

Divide and Conquer

Look at the division problems. For each question, write *dividend, divisor*, or *quotient*, and then write the remainder. If there is no remainder, write *no remainder*.

1. $27 \div 4 = 6 \text{ R } 3$

   What is 27? ______________

   What is 4? ______________

   What is 6 R 3? ______________

   What is the remainder? ______________

2. $36 \div 4 = 9$

   What is the remainder? ______________

   What is 9? ______________

   What is 4? ______________

   What is 36? ______________

3. $71 \div 8 = 8 \text{ R } 7$

   What is 71? ______________

   What is the remainder? ______________

   What is 8 R 7? ______________

   What is 8? ______________

4. $126 \div 6 = 21$

   What is 6? ______________

   What is 126? ______________

   What is 21? ______________

   What is the remainder? ______________

Name ______________________________ Date ____________________

Fractions and Decimals

Choose a word from the box, and label each underlined part.

fraction	denominator	decimal number	numerator

1. $\underline{4.25}$ ____________________

2. $\frac{5}{\underline{6}}$ ____________________

3. $\frac{7}{\underline{8}}$ ____________________

4. $\frac{\underline{2}}{3}$ ____________________

Match each decimal to a fraction.

5. 4.75 **A.** $10\frac{85}{100}$

6. 8.2 **B.** $4\frac{3}{4}$

7. 10.85 **C.** $8\frac{20}{100}$

8. 33.352 **D.** $33\frac{352}{1,000}$

Name ____________________ Date ____________________

Percents and Their Equivalents

Determine if the fractions are equivalent. Write *yes* or *no*.

1 __________

$\frac{2}{8}$

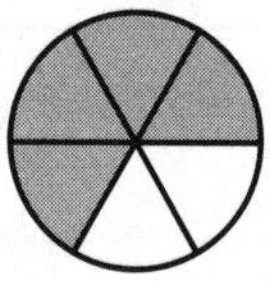

$\frac{4}{6}$

2 __________

$\frac{3}{6}$

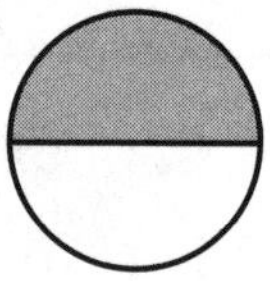

$\frac{1}{2}$

Find equivalent fractions, decimals, or percents to complete the table.

Fraction	Decimal	Percent
$\frac{1}{5}$		20%
	0.50	
$\frac{5}{8}$		62.5%
		35%
	0.70	

Name ______________________________ Date ____________________

Addition Vocabulary and Ratios

Look **at the underlined number. Write *addend* or *sum*.**

1. $34 + \underline{59} = 93$ ____________________

2. $\underline{\frac{1}{4}} + \frac{5}{4} = \frac{6}{4}$ ____________________

3. $2.5 + 9.2 = \underline{11.7}$ ____________________

4. $\underline{12} + 36 = 48$ ____________________

5. $598 + 122 = \underline{720}$ ____________________

6. $\frac{6}{11} = \frac{4}{11} + \underline{\frac{2}{11}}$ ____________________

7. $\underline{3.7} + 7.3 = 11$ ____________________

8. $\underline{708} = 107 + 601$ ____________________

9. $\frac{5}{7} = \underline{\frac{3}{7}} + \frac{2}{7}$ ____________________

10. $6.54 + 3.21 = \underline{9.75}$ ____________________

Write ***addition, ratio*** **or** ***both.***

11. $5 + 3 = 8$ ____________________

12. $\frac{3}{5} + \frac{1}{5} = \frac{4}{5}$ ____________________

13. $\frac{6}{11}$ ____________________

14. $11.45 + 1.33 = 12.78$ ____________________

Name ______________________ Date ______________

Reciprocals and Inverses

Write **the reciprocal (multiplicative inverse) and the additive inverse for each number.**

	Reciprocal	Additive Inverse
1. $\frac{4}{5}$		
2. 92		
3. $-\frac{3}{4}$		
4. 150		
5. $-\frac{9}{13}$		
6. 6		
7. 22		
8. −8		
9. $\frac{5}{6}$		
10. 3		

Name ______________________________ Date ____________________

Expressions and Equations

Look at the underlined part. Write *expression* or *equation*.

1. $\underline{2x} + 1 = 7$ ____________________

2. $\underline{8 + x} = 2y$ ____________________

3. $\underline{14x - \frac{1}{2}x = 27}$ ____________________

4. $\underline{9x = 18}$ ____________________

5. $\underline{7 - n + 3x} = 11$ ____________________

Evaluate the expression.

6. $3 + 4$ ____________________

7. $30 - (3 \times 5)$ ____________________

8. $(4 \times 3) - 9$ ____________________

9. $44 - 11$ ____________________

10. $24 - (6 \times 4)$ ____________________

Name ______________________ Date ______________

Function Tables

Complete the table.

Function: $x \times 10¢ = y$

Number of Bananas *(x)*	Total Cost of Bananas *(y)*
1	
2	
3	
4	
5	50¢
6	
7	
8	

Each peach costs 25¢. Write a function for the cost of peaches. Create a table.

Function: ______________

Number of Peaches *(x)*	Total Cost of Peaches *(y)*
1	
2	
3	
4	
5	
6	
7	
8	

Name ______________________________ Date ____________________

Graphing Variables

Complete the table.

<u>**Function:**</u> $x \times 7¢ = y$

Number of Oranges *(x)*	Total Cost of Oranges *(y)*
1	
2	
3	
4	
5	35¢
6	
7	
8	

Write the ordered pairs.

____

____

____

____

____

____

____

____

Plot the points on the coordinate grid.

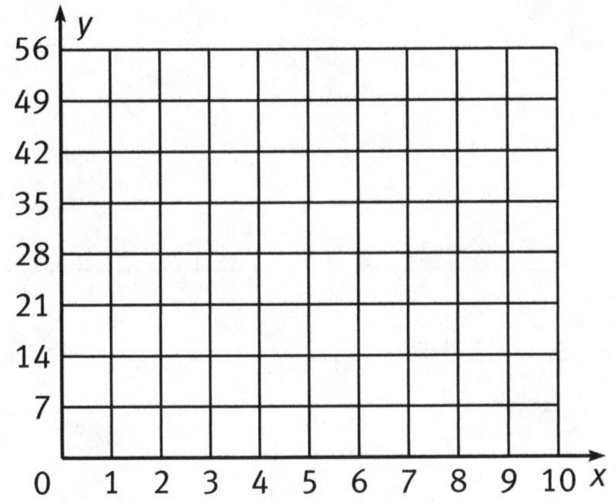

Name ______________________ Date ______________

Vertical, Horizontal, or Slope?

Label the *x*-axis and *y*-axis for each coordinate grid. Then complete each task.

1. Draw a line that has slope.

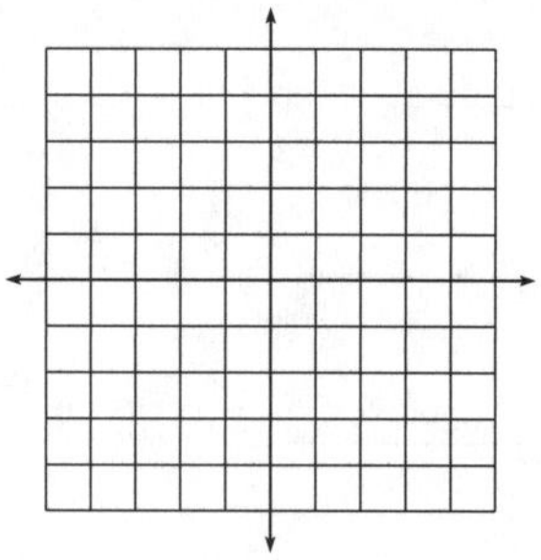

2. Draw a vertical line.

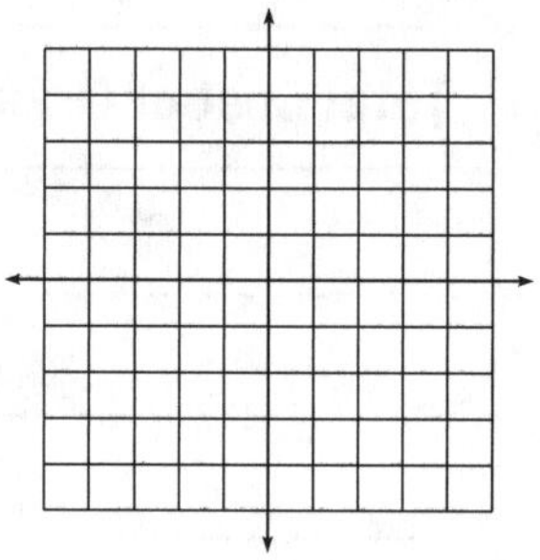

What does x equal?

____

3. Draw a horizontal line.

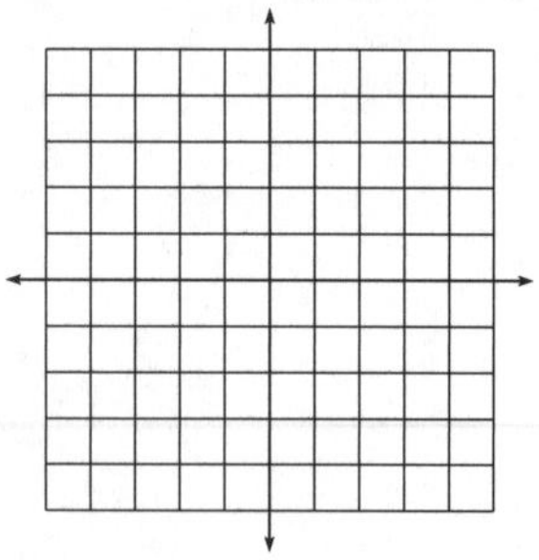

What does y equal?

____

4. Draw a graph for the function $x + 2 = y$. Create ordered pairs, plot the points, and draw the line.

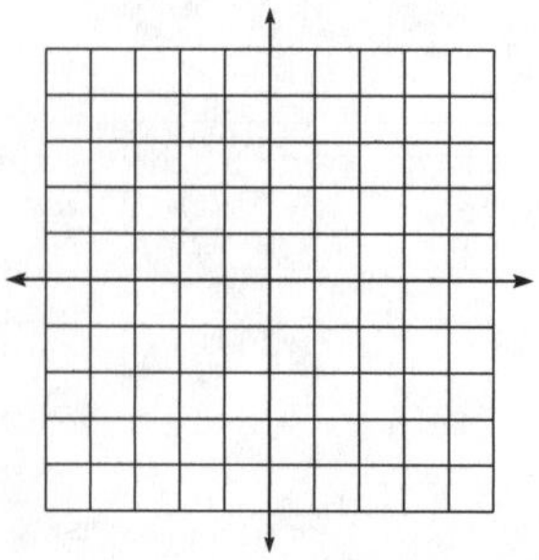

Name ______________________ Date ______________________

You Are My Match If...

Cut out the cards. Each student receives 5 cards. One student at a time, say "You are my match if you have ______________."

The reciprocal of 7	The opposite of $\frac{1}{4}$	$3(x + 1)$	6^2	$\frac{6}{5}$
$3(x - 2)$	$3x + 3$	9	The opposite of -64	36
$9y + 27$	$-\frac{1}{4}$	The reciprocal of $\frac{5}{6}$	$\frac{1}{7}$	4
The square root of 81	64	The square root of 16	$3x - 6$	$9(y + 3)$

Name ______________________ Date ______________________

Linear Equations and Variables

Write the answer to each question.

1. $5x = y$

   What are the variables? ______________________

   Is this a linear equation? ______________________

2. $y = x^2$

   What are the variables? ______________________

   Is this a linear equation? ______________________

3. $a \times (b + c) = (a \times b) + (a \times c)$

   What are the variables? ______________________

   Is this a linear equation? ______________________

4. $12x + 2 = y - 2$

   What are the variables? ______________________

   Is this a linear equation? ______________________

5. $15m \times 1 = 15m$

   What is the variable? ______________________

   Is this a linear equation? ______________________

Letter to Home

Dear Parents,

Welcome to our classroom! Participation in your child's education would be greatly appreciated. You are an important part of making sure that your child is successful in school. Not only would I appreciate your help, but I know that your child would as well.

There are many ways that you can participate and become involved in the classroom. You could help during reading time, writing time, or with math, science, or social studies. If you are talented in music, art, physical education, or have other special talents, your help in any of those areas would be valuable. I could also use help making copies, preparing materials for class, or correcting papers.

If you are not fluent in English, that is not a problem. I will find a interpreter to help us communicate effectively, perhaps even your child can help. Language should not be a barrier to your coming in and participating in your child's education.

Thank you in advance for your time and effort. I look forward to having you help and participate with us this year!

Sincerely,

Letter to Home

Arabic

الآباء الأعزاء،

مرحبًا بكم في قاعتنا الدراسية! ونقدر لكم المشاركة في تعليم طفلكم. فأنتم تمثلون دورًا هامًا في ضمان نجاح طفلكم في المدرسة. ولست وحدي من يقدر مساعدتكم, بل إنني على يقين أن طفلكم سيكن لكم كل تقدير.

هناك طرق عديدة للمشاركة والمساهمة في القاعات الدراسية. فيمكنكم تقديم المساعدة أثناء وقت القراءة أو وقت الكتابة أو في الرياضيات أو العلوم أو الدراسات الاجتماعية. وإذا كنتم موهوبين في الموسيقى أو الفنون الجميلة أو التربية البدنية أو لديكم مواهب خاصة أخرى، فسوف يكون للمساعدة في أي من هذه المجالات نفع عظيم. ويمكنني أيضًا الاستفادة من مساعدتكم في عمل النسخ أو إعداد المواد التدريسية أو تصحيح الأوراق.

وإذا كنتم لا تتحدثون الإنجليزية بطلاقة، فلا يمثل ذلك أدنى مشكلة. فسوف أحضر مترجمًا لمساعدتنا في التواصل بفعالية، وربما يستطيع طفلكم المساعدة في ذلك. وبذلك لا ينبغي أن تكون اللغة عائقًا أمام قدومكم ومشاركتكم في تعليم طفلكم.

أشكركم مقدمًا على وقتكم وجهدكم. وأتطلع إلى رؤية مساعدتكم ومشاركتكم معنا هذا العام!

وتفضلوا بقبول فائق الاحترام،

Letter to Home

Creole

Paran,

Nou byen kontan wè w nan klas nou an! Nou apresye patisipasyon w nan edikasyon pitit ou anpil anpil. Ou se yon manm kle ki la pou asire pitit ou jwenn siksè nan afè lekòl li. Non sèlman m ap apresye patisipasyon ou, men mwen konnen pitit ap apresye patisipasyon w tou.

Gen plizyè fason ou kab patisipe nan travay klas la ap fè. Ou kab ede nan klas pandan y ap fè kou lekti, kou ekriti, kou matematik, kou syans ak kou syans sosyal. Si ou gen talan nan mizik, nan travay atistik, nan espò, oubyen ou gen nenpòt lòt talan espesyal, epi si ou kab bay kout men nan nenpòt kategori sa yo sa ap ede nou anpil. Kèk fwa mwen bezwen moun ede mwen fè fotokopi, oubyen prepare materyèl pou klas la, oubyen korije papye.

Si w pa fin twò maton nan Angle, pa gen pwoblèm nan sa. M ap chèche yon entèprèt pou ede nou kominike ansanm, pitit ou kab menm ede nou. Pa kite jan w pale lang nan anpeche w vin patisipe nan edikasyon pitit ou.

Mèsi davans pou tan ou ak efò w ap fè. M ap tann ou vin patisipe pou w ban nou yon kout men ane sa!

Mwen salye ou,

Letter to Home

Hmong

Nyob zoo cov Niam cov Txiv,

Zoo siab txais tos nej rau hauv peb hoob kawm ntawv! Peb xav kom nej nrog peb koom tes pab qhia ntawv rau nej tus me nyuam. Nej yog ib co tseem ceeb uas yuav pab nrog xyuas kom nej tus me nyuam kawm tau ntaub ntawv zoo. Tsis yog kuv ib leeg xwb uas yuav ris nej txiaj rau tej kev pab no, tiam sis kuv paub tias nej tus me nyuam yuav ris nej txiaj ib yam.

Muaj ntau yam uas nej ua tau kom thiaj nrog peb koom tes qhia ntawv hauv hoob kawm ntawv. Nej pab tau thaum lub sij hawm nyeem ntawv, sau ntawv, los sis lub sij hawm ua leb, kawm txuj ci, los sis keeb kwm tib neeg. Yog tias nej txawj nkauj, teeb duab, qhia kev kom tes taw, los sis muaj lwm yam kev txawj, peb yuav zoo siab heev yog tias nej pab tau peb rau tej ntawd. Kuv kuj xav tau kev pab luam ntawv, npaj khoom rau txoj kev qhia ntawv, los sis kuaj ntawv thiab.

Yog tias nej tsis txawj hais lus As Kiv zoo, tsis ua li cas. Kuv mam li nrhiav kom tau ib tug neeg txhais lus kom peb thiaj li sib tham tau zoo, thiab tej zaum nej tus me nyuam pab txhais lus tau thiab. Qhov uas tsis paub lus As Kiv zoo yuav tsum tsis txhob ua rau nej xav tias nej nrog tsis tau peb koom tes pab qhia ntawv rau nej tus me nyuam.

Ua tsaug ntau rau nej lub caij thiab lub dag zog. Kuv cia siab rau nej tej kev pab thiab tej kev koom peb xyoo no!

Sau npe,

Letter to Home

Japanese

保護者各位

私たちのクラスルームへようこそ！皆様方が子ども達の教育に関われることに感謝いたします。皆様は子ども達の学習成果を確認する上で重要な役割を持っています。私が皆様の参加に感謝するのみならず、子ども達も同様に感謝することと思います。

クラスルームに参加し、関わりを持つ方法はいくつかあります。読書や作文の時間、または算数、科学、社会科の時間にお手伝いしていただけます。あるいは、音楽、芸術、体育、またはその他の特殊技能や知識をお持ちなら、その分野でのサポートも貴重です。コピーやクラスのための資料作成、添削などのお手伝をいいただく場合もあります。

英語が不自由でも、心配は要りません。通訳の方に間に入っていただくこともできますし、または、子ども達に手伝っていただくこともできます。教育に参加していただくのに、言語が障害になることはありません。

皆様の貴重な時間と尽力に前もってお礼を申し上げます。これからの皆様の力添えとご参加を大いに期待しております。

敬具

Letter to Home

Khmer

គោរពជូនមាតាបិតាសិស្ស,

ថ្នាក់រៀនយើងខ្ញុំសូមស្វាគមន៍! ការរួមចំណែកក្នុងការសិក្សាអប់រំរបស់កូនអ្នកនឹងត្រូវទទួលការអបអរយ៉ាងក្រៃលែង ។ អ្នកគឺជាផ្នែកមួយដ៏សំខាន់ ក្នុងការធ្វើឲ្យកូនអ្នកមានជោគជ័យក្នុងការសិក្សា ។ មិនត្រឹមតែខ្ញុំទេដែលអបអរចំពោះការជួយរបស់អ្នក ប៉ុន្តែខ្ញុំថែមទាំងដឹងថា កូនអ្នកក៏អបអរផងដែរ ។

មានមធ្យោបាយជាច្រើនដែលអ្នកអាចចូលរួមនិងរួមចំណែកក្នុងថ្នាក់រៀនរបស់កូនអ្នក ។ អ្នកអាចជួយក្នុងពេលអាន, ពេលសរសេរ, ឬការធ្វើលំហាត់គណិតសាស្ត្រ, វិទ្យាសាស្ត្រ, ឬ សង្គមវិទ្យា ។ បើអ្នកមានទេពកោសល្យខាងភ្លេង, គំនូរ, កីឡា, ឬមានទេពកោសល្យពិសេសផ្សេងទៀត, ការជួយរបស់អ្នកក្នុងផ្នែកណាមួយនោះ នឹងមានគុណប្រយោជន៍ ។ ខ្ញុំក៏អាចត្រូវការអ្នកឲ្យជួយថតចំឡងឯកសារ, រៀបចំសម្ភារៈសំរាប់ថ្នាក់រៀន, ឬកែលំហាត់ផងដែរ ។

បើអ្នកមិនសូវចេះភាសាអង់គ្លេស វាមិនជាបញ្ហាឡើយ ។ ខ្ញុំនឹងរកអ្នកបកប្រែដើម្បីជួយឲ្យយើងទំនាក់ទំនងគ្នាដោយប្រសិទ្ធិភាព, ប្រហែលកូនអ្នកក៏អាចជួយបានដែរ ។ ភាសាមិនគួរជាឧបសគ្គដល់ការរួមចំណែកក្នុងការសិក្សាអប់រំរបស់កូនអ្នកឡើយ ។

សូមអរគុណទុកជាមុនចំពោះពេលវេលានិងការខិតខំប្រឹងប្រែងរបស់អ្នក ។ ខ្ញុំរង់ចាំទទួលជំនួយ និងការចូលរួមរបស់អ្នកជាមួយយើងក្នុងឆ្នាំសិក្សានេះ!

ដោយក្តីគោរពរាប់អាន,

Letter to Home

Korean

학부모님께,

저희 교실에 오신것을 환영합니다! 자녀 교육을 위한 부모님들의 참여에 매우 감사드립니다. 부모의 협조는 자녀들의 학업적 성공에 있어 매우 중요한 요소 입니다. 저뿐만 아니라 귀댁의 자녀들도 부모님들의 참여를 기뻐할 것입니다.

귀하가 수업에 참여 하거나 도울 수 있는 일은 아주 많습니다. 읽기 타임, 쓰기 타임, 또는 수학, 과학, 그리고 사회과 과목등에 도움을 주실 수 있습니다. 만약 음악, 미술, 체육 등 기타 특기를 소지하고 계신다면 그런 분야에 있어 매우 소중한 도움을 줄 수 있을 것입니다. 저 또한 카피를 하거나 수업을 위한 자료를 준비하거나 시험지를 채점하는 등 여러가지 도움을 필요로 합니다.

영어를 잘 못 하셔도 문제가 없습니다. 우리가 효과적으로 의사 소통을 할 수 있도록 번역사를 찾거나 혹은 귀하의 자녀가 도움을 줄 수도 있습니다. 귀하가 자녀의 교육에 참여 하는데 언어가 장애물이. 되서는 않됩니다.

귀하의 시간과 노력에 미리 감사를 드립니다. 올 한해 귀하의 도움과 참여를 기대합니다!

감사합니다,

Letter to Home

Russian

Дорогие родители,

Добро пожаловать в наш класс! Мы будем очень признательны за участие в обучении Вашего ребенка. Ваша роль является очень важной для обеспечения успехов Вашего ребенка в школе. Не только я буду признателен за Вашу помощь. Я уверен в том, что Ваш ребенок тоже будет Вам благодарен.

Есть много способов того, как Вы сможете принимать участие в жизни класса. Вы можете помочь во время чтения, письменных занятий, или с математикой, другими точными или гуманитарными предметами. Если у Вас есть способности к музыке, искусству, физическому воспитанию, или другие таланты, Ваша помощь в этих областях будет очень ценной. Я могу также использовать помощь в копировании, подготовке материалов для класса или проверке домашних заданий.

Если Вы не очень хорошо знаете английский, это не проблема. Я найду переводчика, который поможет нам эффективно общаться, возможно даже, что Ваш ребенок сможет нам помочь. Язык не должен быть барьером для Ваших посещений и участия в обучении Вашего ребенка.

Заранее благодарю Вас за Ваше время и усилия. Я надеюсь на Вашу помощь и участие в этом году!

Искренне Ваш,

Letter to Home

Chinese

尊敬的学生家长：

欢迎来到我们的教室！非常希望您能参与到您孩子的教育中来。您是保证孩子取得学业成功的重要因素。我和孩子都会感谢您的帮助。

您可通过多种方式参与教学工作。您可在阅读课、作文课或者数学、自然科学、社会学科方面提供帮助。如果您有音乐、美术、体育或者其他方面的才能，也可在这些方面提供宝贵的帮助。我还需要在复印材料、准备教学材料、批改考卷方面获得帮助。

即便您不能讲流利的英语也没关系。我会找一位口译员帮助我们更好地交流，也许您的孩子就能帮助我们。语言不应成为您参与孩子教育的障碍。

特此提前感谢您所付出的时间和努力。我期盼能得到您的帮助，请今年就参与我们的工作！

此致敬礼

Letter to Home

Somali

Gacaliyeyaal Waalid,

Ku soo dhawaada fasalkayaga! Waxa si weyn laydinka mahadcelin doonaa ka qaybgalka waxbarashada ilmihiina. Waxa aad qayb lagama maarmaan ah ka tihiin sidii loo sugi lahaa in ilmihiinu ku guuleysto dugsiga. Si weyn baan idiinka mahadcelin doonaa gargaarkiina, sidoo kale waxa aan ogahay in ilmihiina laftiisu idiinka mahadcelin doono.

Waxa jira siyaabo badan oo aad uga qaybgali kartaan hawlaha fasalka. Waxa aad gargaar bixin kartaan wakhtiga akhriska, wakhtiga qorista, ama waxa aad gargaar ka geysan kartaan xisaabta, sayniska, ama culaanta bulshada. Haddii aad hibo u leedihiin muusigga, farshaxanka, aqoonta jimicsiga, ama aad leedihiin aqoon kale oo gaar ah, waxa qiime yeelan doonaa wixii aad gargaar bixisaan ee ku saabsan aqoontaa. Waxa kale oo i anfici kara gargaarka xagga sameynta koobiyada, diyaarinta alaabta fasalka, ama sixidda waraaqaha.

Haddii aanad aad u oqoon ku hadalka Ingiriisiga, taasi ma laha wax dhib ah. Waxa aannu raadin doonaa turjubaan inaga gargaari doona isgaadhsiinta; xiitaa waxa laga yaabaa in ilmahiinu ina gargaaro. Waa inaan afla'antu is hortaagin imaanshihiina iyo ka-qaybgalkiina waxbarashada ilmihiina.

Hormaris ahaan waad ku mahadsantihiin wakhtigiina iyo dadaalkiina. Waxa aan dhawrayaa in aan helo gargaarkiina oo aad nagala qaybgashaan hawlaha sannadkan!

Si gacalnimo leh,

Letter to Home

Tagalog

Mahal na mga Magulang,

Maligayang pagdating sa aming klase! Ang pakikilahok sa edukasyon ng inyong anak ay lubos naming pinahahalagahan. Kayo po ay isang mahalagang bahagi upang masiguro ang tagumpay ng inyong anak sa kanyang pag-aaral. Hindi lang ako ang magpapahalaga ng inyong tulong, ngunit batid ko na pati na rin ang inyong anak.

Maraming paraan kung paano kayo makakasali at magiging abala sa silid-aralan. Maaari kayong tumulong sa oras ng pagbasa, pagsulat, o sa matematika, agham, o araling panlipunan. Kung kayo ay may talento sa musika, sining, araling pampalakasan, o mayroon pang mga natatanging talento, ang inyong tulong sa mga nabanggit na aralin ay napakahalaga. Kailangan ko rin po ng tulong sa paggawa ng mga kopya, paghahanda ng mga materyales para sa klase, o pagtsetsek ng mga papel.

Kung kayo ay hindi matatas o mahusay sa pagsasalita ng Ingles, ito po ay hindi isang problema. Ako po ay maghahanap ng tagasalin upang tulungan kayong makipag-usap ng mabuti, maaaring makatulong din ang inyong anak. Ang lengguwahe ay hindi dapat maging isang sagabal sa inyong pagpunta rito at pakikilahok sa edukasyon ng inyong anak.

Paunang pasasalamat sa inyong panahon at pagpupunyagi. Ako po ay umaasa sa inyong tulong at pakikilahok sa amin ngayong taon!

Lubos na sumasainyo,

extend
face
factors
factor pair
flat surface
fraction
function
greater than
greatest
height
histogram
hundredths
identity property of multiplication
impossible
input
input/output table
least
length
less than
line plot
mean
median
millions
mode
multiply
negative number
net
number line
numerator
outcome
output
pair
place value
plot
population
predict
probability
product
quotient
R
range
remainder
right angle
round
rounding
ruler
same-step pattern
sample
space figure
spatial visualization
subtraction
sum
surface area
tenths
variable
volume
whole
width
zero property of multiplication

Level H

acute angle
addend
angle
area
associative property
bar graph
base
biased
bilateral symmetry
common denominator
commutative property
constant
coordinate grid
decimal
decimal number
decimal point
denominator
difference
digit
distributive property
divide
dividend
divisor
edge
equivalent
estimate
exponent
face
factors
fraction
function
function rule
histogram
identity property
input
integer
interior angle
inverse operations
line graphs
line plot
linear equation
mean
median
mode
numerator
obtuse angle
one-hundred percent
order of operations
ordered pair
output
percent
polygon
population
probability
product
quotient
random
range
regular polygon
remainder
representative
right angle
rotation
rotational symmetry
round
sample
significant digit
sum
symmetry
theoretical
thousandth
tree diagram
variable
vertex
volume
whole
x-axis
y-axis

Level I

acute angle
additive inverse
algebraic expression
algorithm
angle
area
bar graph
circle
circle graph
circumference
complementary angles
constant
coordinate grid
decimal
decimal point
denominator
dependent event
diameter
equation
equivalent
equivalent fraction
factors
fraction
function
GCF
greatest common factor
histogram
hundredths
independent event
integer
inverse operation
LCD
LCM
least common denominator
least common multiple
line graph
mean
median
mixed number
mode
negative number
numerator
obtuse angle
ordered pair
outlier
parallelogram
percent
place value
positive number
prime factorization
prime number
prism
probability
proportion
pyramid
quotient
radius
random sample
range
rate
ratio
reciprocal
right angle
sample
scale
scale drawing
supplementary angles
surface area
tenths
thousandths
triangle
unit rate
variable
volume
whole number
x-axis
y-axis

Level J

absolute value
algebraic sentence
area
axes
bar graph
box-and-whisker plot
coefficient
complementary events
congruent figures
constant
cubic unit
decimal
decimal point
dependent event
equation
equivalent
equivalent fractions
exponent
expression
factors
fraction
function
greater than
hypotenuse
improper fraction
independent event
inequality
integer
less than
line graph
linear function
mean
median
mixed number
mode
negative number
nonlinear function
not equal to
number line
odds
ordered pair
outcome
outlier
percent
positive number
probability
proportion
Pythagorean theorem
quadrant
range
rate
ratio
rational number
reciprocal
reflection
right angle
scale
scientific notation
similar figures
slope
square
square root
surface area
trial
variable
volume
x-axis
y-axis

Algebra Readiness

addend
addition
algorithm
associative
balanced equation
commutative
constant
coordinate grid
decimal
decimal number
decimal point
denominator
digit
dimensional analysis
distributive
dividend
divisor
equal
equation
equivalent fractions
evaluate
exponent
expression
factor
fraction
function
graph
greater than
horizontal
hypotenuse
inequality
integer
inverse
less than
line
line segment
linear function
mixed number
multiply
negative number
numerator
operation
opposite
order of operations
ordered pair
parentheses
percent
place value
plot the points
positive numbers
prime number
product
Pythagorean theorem
quotient
rate
ratio
rational number
reciprocal
remainder
right angle
simplify
slope
solution set
subtract
sum
table
unit rate
unknown
variable
vertical
x-axis
y-axis

Student Assessment Record

		Individual Oral Assessment				Activity completed	Final Assessment			
		Score	Beginning English Learner	Intermediate English Learner	Advanced English Learner		Score	Beginning English Learner	Intermediate English Learner	Advanced English Learner
Unit 1	Chapter 1	13				4				
	Chapter 2	13				4				
	Chapter 3	13				4				
	Chapter 4	13				4				
Unit 2	Chapter 5	13				4				
	Chapter 6	13				4				
	Chapter 7	13				4				
	Chapter 8	13				4				
Unit 3	Chapter 9	13				4				
	Chapter 10	13				4				
	Chapter 11	13				4				
	Chapter 12	13				4				
Unit 4	Chapter 13	13				4				
	Chapter 14	13				4				
	Chapter 15	13				4				
	Chapter 16	13				4				
Unit 5	Chapter 17	13				4				
	Chapter 18	13				4				
	Chapter 19	13				4				
	Chapter 20	13				4				
Unit 6	Chapter 21	13				4				
	Chapter 22	13				4				
	Chapter 23	13				4				
	Chapter 24	13				4				